The U.S. Government Response to Terrorism

Also of Interest

Victims of Terrorism, edited by Frank M. Ochberg and David A. Soskis

International Terrorism: An Annotated Bibliography and Research Guide, Augustus R. Norton and Martin H. Greenberg

**Terrorism and Hostage Negotiations,* Abraham H. Miller

**Terrorism: Theory and Practice,* edited by Yonah Alexander, David Carlton, and Paul Wilkinson

Self-Determination: National, Regional, and Global Dimensions, edited by Yonah Alexander and Robert A. Friedlander

Insurgency in the Modern World, edited by Bard E. O'Neill, William R. Heaton, and Donald J. Alberts

Global Human Rights: Public Policies, Comparative Measures, and NGO Strategies, edited by Ved P. Nanda, James R. Scarritt, and George W. Shepherd, Jr.

**Contemporary International Law: A Concise Introduction,* Werner Levi

Arms Transfers to the Third World: The Military Buildup in Less Industrial Countries, edited by Uri Ra'anan, Robert L. Pfaltzgraff, Jr., and Geoffrey Kemp

Terrorism and Global Security: The Nuclear Threat, Louis Rene Beres

Arms Transfers, Economic Growth, and Political Stability in Africa: The Risks of Military Development, Bruce E. Arlinghaus

**The United Nations and a Just World Order,* edited by Richard Falk, Samuel Kim, Donald McNemar, and Saul Mendlovitz

National Security Crisis Forecasting and Management From Basic Research to Operational Use, edited by Gerald W. Hopple, Stephen J. Andriole, and Amos Freedy

*Available in hardcover and paperback.

Westview Special Studies in National and International Terrorism

The U.S. Government Response to Terrorism: In Search of an Effective Strategy
William Regis Farrell

This book examines the organizational problems faced by the U.S. government in developing an effective strategy to counter terrorism and presents a detailed history of U.S. counter-terrorist policy since 1972.

Dr. Farrell offers a working definition of terrorism, reviews its international, transnational, nonterritorial, and domestic forms, then focuses on the activities of those U.S. government agencies directly concerned with the prevention or neutralization of terrorism. Critical of existing programs and of the fact that counter-terrorist activities seem to have a low priority among the duties of the relevant agencies' key executives, he concludes that the development of a clear, reasonable, and effective strategy against terrorism has been unnecessarily delayed. He is doubtful whether, even now, a satisfactory arrangement has been achieved.

Beyond looking strictly at governmental agency responses to terrorism, Dr. Farrell considers the sociological, legal, and operational factors that would be brought into play should military forces be employed to quell a terrorist attack and also addresses the nature and extent of the terrorist threat to U.S. businesses.

Dr. Farrell (Lt.Col., USAF) has been involved in counter-intelligence since 1966 and has conducted research at the U.S. Naval War College on the U.S. government's efforts to combat terrorism. He is now deputy chief, Security Division, Organization of Joint Chiefs of Staff, Washington, D.C.

For Marabeth, Kirsten, and Brendan
With Love and Grateful Appreciation

The U.S. Government Response to Terrorism: In Search of an Effective Strategy

William Regis Farrell

Westview Press / Boulder, Colorado

Westview Special Studies in National and International Terrorism

Copyright © 1982 by Westview Press, Inc.

Published in 1982 in the United States of America by
     Westview Press, Inc.
     5500 Central Avenue
     Boulder, Colorado 80301
     Frederick A. Praeger, President and Publisher

Library of Congress Catalog Card Number 82-50665
ISBN 0-86531-402-0

Composition for this book was provided by the author
Printed and bound in the United States of America

Contents

List of Tables and Figures viii
Preface ix

1. The Setting 1

2. Terrorism Is...? 6

3. The Organizational Perspective 19

4. Governmental Structure to
   Counter Terrorism 32

5. Aspects of Military Involvement 49

6. The Need for Organizational Response 69

7. How the Organizations Responded 96

8. Conclusions 119

Bibliography 129
Index 135

Tables and Figures

Tables

6.1 Terrorist Activity in North America, 1970-1979 . . 71

6.2 Assassinations, 1970-1979 72

6.3 Kidnappings, 1970-1979 73

6.4 Bombings, 1970-1979 74

6.5 Hijackings, 1970-1979 75

6.6 Facility Attacks, 1970-1979 76

6.7 Terrorist Activity for 1979 78

6.8 Terrorist Activity for 1980 80

Figures

4.1 Organization for Response to Terrorist
     Incidents, Carter Administration 38

4.2 Organization for Antiterrorism Planning,
     Coordination, and Policy Formulation,
     Carter Administration 39

Preface

Terrorism is mesmerizing. Mention of the term con-
jures up images of masked gunmen, bombs exploding, and
planes being hijacked. The decade of the 1970s saw over
8,000 acts of terrorism carried out around the globe.
People were riveted to their televisions and radios
awaiting news from the Olympic village at Munich, Lod
Airport in Tel Aviv, and the embassies in Bogota and
Teheran.

Terrorism is an unacceptable affront to society,
disrupting the very foundations upon which society is
based. To counter this threat, governments, through their
established organizations, attempt to provide the needed
security for their people. And the number of public statements, organizational charts, and pronouncements of policy
could well give rise to the notion that governments are
fully capable of meeting the threat. But are they?

This book goes beyond the rhetoric to the very core
of the U.S. government's counterterrorist effort. Through
a comprehensive examination of the press and public testimony and a very extensive series of interviews, the true
measure of the antiterror program is revealed.

Appearances and substance are not always the same.
The Cabinet Committee to Combat Terrorism, the Executive
Committee on Terrorism, the Presidential proclamations,
Presidential Decision memorandums, the Omnibus Antiterrorism Act, as well as the numerous military units identified as "having counterterrorist capability," lead one to
believe that the U.S. government has seriously addressed
the issue and developed an adequate response. However,
the reader will discover, as various government organizations are examined, that a clear, understandable, and
effective strategy to counter terrorism has only evolved
slowly, if at all. As we enter the 1980s, it is debatable
whether a highly workable arrangement has yet been achieved.

With any research project the numbers of people aiding in its successful completion are legion. This effort
is no exception. The Center for Advanced Research, Naval
War College, and Dr. Robert F. Delaney allowed me the time

to complete this project and provided much appreciated support as the foundations of this study were laid.

Many present or former members of the following government agencies provided generously of their time often, understandably, on a nonattributable basis: Staff of the National Security Council, Department of State, Office of the Secretary of Defense and the Joint Chiefs of Staff, Central Intelligence Agency, Department of Justice and the Federal Bureau of Investigation, Department of Energy, Department of the Treasury, Department of Transportation including the Federal Aviation Administration, and the U.S. Coast Guard. Various staff members on several U.S. Senate and Congressional committees provided data and a much needed understanding of the ways of Capitol Hill.

I am indebted to Roy Tucker and Dr. Charles Russell, of Risks International, Inc., for advice and access to their extensive data base on international terrorist incidents.

To members of the faculty of the University of Michigan, especially Dr. Allen S. Whiting, who followed closely the development of this book, Drs. Harold K. Jacobson, Milton Heumann, and Bradford Perkins, I am most appreciative for constructive criticism, continuing guidance, and needed encouragement. And to Dr. Catherine McArdle Kelleher—a special person who has the wonderful ability to be there, to chastise or to inspire—goes my heartfelt gratitude.

A special recognition is needed for those who provided editorial and typing support. Without their efforts, all would have been in vain.

Last, but certainly not least, a word of sincere thanks to my friends, who provided needed support during the many times of travail.

W.R.F.

1
The Setting

This book will, from an organizational perspective, concern itself with the countering of transnational terrorism. Terrorists pose a potential threat to the nation and effective organizational countermeasures are essential for the maintenance of public order and political stability.[1]

Terrorism is directed against institutions or personages holding social and/or political power. It is evident that the nature of these targets determines the effectiveness and the means of the attack. The strength of a society, or more particularly a government within a society, depends in part upon the ability of key agencies to transmit or allocate societal and consensual values without distortion.[2] This requires that these institutions be secure in the sense of maintaining, with public approbation, the intellectual and material resources necessary to counter serious threats from both within and without.

Security maintenance becomes increasingly difficult as powerful forces -- urbanization, industrialization, technological changes, popular and legal alienation, disruption or displacement due to war -- place strains upon the system. If the strain becomes severe, discordant groups such as terrorists find fertile fields for exploitation. As dissatisfied groups feel their ties to the community breaking down, they seek to unite in other ways. As links with church, family or government weaken, individuals may search out new social and symbolic arrangements as substitutes for those accepted in the past.[3] Governmental organizations once capable of fulfilling these needs become much less effective in dealing with the situation. The vacuum thus created is filled by groups that provide surrogate means of social participation.[4]

This book will concern itself only peripherally with specific groups, i.e., terrorists who seek to fill the void caused by perceived severe governmental inadequacies. In the main, it will address the tremendous problem faced by the U.S. government, as a structure of organizations, in coping with their potential activity.

In a democracy the methods of action available to leaders are limited. The use of a secret police, censorship, or denial of the right of free speech or assembly will not be tolerated. Since the goal of the government is the defense of certain values, the weapons used against the terrorist must be fashioned to preserve these values in the course of their defense. An understanding of the structure of organizations, as channels of policy actions, will aid greatly in comprehending the difficulty in countering the serious threat posed by transnational terrorism.

To date, the threat posed by terrorists in the United States is not primarily the result of indigenous forces but rather, outside forces seeking to further their particular cause on American soil.[5] The national experience has been limited to groups such as the Weathermen and the Symbionese Liberation Army, both small in number and limited in popular appeal. Such groups are more analagous to tiny gangs of bandits than to serious political movements, despite claims that they are the "vanguard of a people's revolution."[6] However, the activities of certain Puerto Rican national groups bear watching in the future. Social conditions have remained stable enough in the United States that the disruptive appeal has been quite restricted. What made their activities noteworthy and what makes the U.S. a prime target for terrorist activity is the heavy attention given such events by the media. In relying on immediate and extensive coverage by television, radio, and the press for the maximum amount of propagandizing, terrorists can rapidly and effectively reach audiences at home and abroad. This can lead to an enhancement of the effectiveness of their violence by the creation of an emotional state of fear which results in the granting of demands.[7] If the government responds harshly, it may result in sympathy toward the terrorist. Tom Hayden, one of the founders of the Students for a Democratic Society, addressed this very topic when he referred to stern countermeasures by the U.S. government: "The coming of repression will speed up time, making a revolutionary situation more likely -- we are creating an America where it is necessary for the government to rule behind barbed wire.....where it will be necessary for the people to fight back."[8] The careful and judicious handling of terrorist situations is a most demanding task. The suddenness of the terror coupled with the danger of lost lives requires effective countermeasures to be timely and complete. There will be little time for bureaucratic and organizational disputes over jurisdiction as the agencies concerned haggle over the right approach.

At first blush, it may appear that the United States would not be vulnerable to a transnational attack within its borders. However, despite the growth of modern weaponry and the increased sophistication of defense planning, highly industrialized nations remain quite fragile. In fact, the highly technological, exposed, and interdependent automated systems so essential to our modern society provide many prime targets for terrorist groups. Commercial aircraft, natural gas pipelines, electric power grids, offshore oil rigs, and computers storing government and corporate records are examples of sabotage-prone targets whose destruction would have more serious effects than their primary losses would suggest. Social fragility is reflected in the blackout which occurred in New York City on July 13, 1977. The disproportionately high damage caused by uncontrolled looting and arson, resource shortages, and loss of public confidence, attests to urban vulnerability. On that day lightning completely disrupted the Consolidated Edison System, immobilizing ten million people. Subways and elevators came to a halt. Airports and television networks were forced to close down. Thousands of looters surged through the streets, resulting in 3300 arrests and causing injury to nearly 100 policemen. It was estimated that the cost of the damage approached $150 million.[9] If the blackout had lasted four or five days, it is easy to picture New York almost paralyzed with numerous incidents of looting, arson, and panic.

The point here is that an "act of nature" with the aid of human inefficiency produced a two-day siege. Probably a quite small but trained paramilitary force could take the city of New York or any other large metropolitan area off line for considerably longer periods of time.[10] However, despite the magnitude of the threat, only limited countermeasures by the governmental organizations concerned have been undertaken. The objective in undertaking this book is to determine to what degree the lack of development of antiterrorist strategies is due to the structure and functions of organizations themselves. The research will center upon those governmental organizations directly concerned with the prevention and/or neutralization of transnational terrorism targeted within the United States.

Certain key assumptions lie at the foundation of this work:

1. Agencies within the United States have developed plans to detect, prevent, and neutralize terrorist acts, but the plans cross over the jurisdictions of several organizations. Here we have the classic case of the decentralization required

by government running headlong into the requirement of coordination.

2. Such plans have been developed within agencies,
among agencies and by ad hoc groups at the
highest level of decision making -- the National
Security Council.

3. Key personnel in concerned organizations are
extremely worried about the outcome of any
terrorist attack, while appearing to tempt fate
through inaction. But their programs and repertoires make change difficult except at the
margins. Further, other demands upon organizational leaders draw their attention in different
directions, making concentration on one issue
difficult.

4. Bureaucratic and organizational imperatives
common to all agencies -- i.e., factoring of
problems, parochial priorities, goals and the
sequential attention to them, standard operating
procedures, concern for uncertainty, resistance
to change, and much more -- hinder needed
cooperation.

To better appreciate the complexities that confront
organizations, this book will begin with the formulation
of an operational definition of terrorism, highlighting
its many complexities.

NOTES

1. Terrorist activities worldwide increased at a
dramatic rate during 1979 when 2585 significant actions
(i.e., assassinations, kidnappings, hijacking, and bombings) were reported. This compared to a total of 1511
incidents in 1978. Data is based on Executive Risk
Assessment, Vol. 1, no. 12, 1979, prepared by Risks
International, Alexandria, VA. Information available
for 1980 showed no let up.

2. David Easton, Framework of Political Analysis
(Englewood Cliffs, NJ: Prentice-Hall, 1965). The author
distinguishes a political system from all other systems
as one predominately oriented toward the "authoritarian
allocation of values." The values are allotted in three
ways: providing access to some but denying it to others;
depriving a person of a valued thing already possessed;
obstructing the attainment of values. The process of
allocation is binding upon the populace and is in the
form of decrees, rules, laws, and policies which must
meet the demands of the society. Failing this, the political system, if it is to sustain, must be able to
coerce existing support.

3. This was very common for college students during the 1960s and early 1970s. It was not just a phenomenon in the United States but also in Europe and Asia. The educated youth began to question not only their role within a society but also the authority and purpose of the university and the government. Students banded together, often disruptively, in efforts to bring about change. Studies concerning the so-called "student movement" fully document this occurrence. See Edwin Wright Bakke, Revolutionary Democracy (Hamden, CT: Archon Books, 1968). In Japan it has been shown that student activism and the subsequent feelings of alienation were directly related to the rise of a terrorist group, the Japanese Red Army.

4. The failure of governmental organizations to respond to the needs of the people is very much part of world history. It can occur over an extended period such as in China in the nineteenth and twentieth centuries where total decay was replaced with stability only after millions had died and various forms of order were attempted. It may also be more limited and time-specific, such as the kinds that grip societies during a period of modernization. Samuel Huntington, in his work "Civil Violence and the Process of Development," Adelphi Paper no. 83 (London: 1971), suggests that rapid modernization always involves intensified relative deprivation because it widens the gap between the changing aspirations and capabilities of the groups involved. Social mobilization, education, increased opportunities, and governmental and administration resources cannot keep pace with fresh expectations and needs.

5. Hugh David Graham and Ted Robert Gurr, eds., Violence in America (Beverly Hills, CA: Sage Publications, 1979), p. 333.

6. Paul Wilkinson, "Terrorist Movements," Terrorism: Theory and Practice, Yonah Alexander, David Carlton and Paul Wilkinson, eds. (Boulder, CO: Westview Press, 1979), p. 107.

7. Yonah Alexander, "Terrorism and the Media," Ibid., p. 160.

8. Robert Moss, "Urban Guerilla Warfare," American Defense Policy, Richard G. Head and Ervin J. Rokke, eds. (Baltimore: Johns Hopkins University Press, 1973), p. 257.

9. New York Times, July 15, 1977, p. 1: July 22, 1977, p. 12.

10. Robert H. Kupperman, Facing Tomorrow's Terrorist Incident Today (Law Enforcement Assistance Administration, U.S. Department of Justice, Washington, D.C.: October 1977), p. 1.

2
Terrorism Is . . . ?

When we speak of terrorism it is not always clear just what one has in mind. The term has no precise and completely accepted definition. Some countries label those who engage in violent acts against them as terrorists. Freedom fighters rarely label themselves in such a way but they often claim they are subjected to governmental terror. "In short, the definition of terrorism seems to depend on one's point of view -- it is what the 'bad guys' do."[1]

Terrorism is frequently described as mindless, senseless, and irrational violence. However, none of these terms is appropriate. It is not mindless and there is a theory of terrorism that frequently works. Terrorism should be viewed as a means to an end and not an end unto itself. While terrorist activity may appear random, closer examination reveals that terrorism has objectives. Attacks are often carefully choreographed to attract media attention. The holding of hostages serves to increase the drama, especially if their being killed is a possibility. Terrorism is aimed at the people watching and, in this sense, "terrorism is theater."[2]

While the term "terrorism" is often indiscriminately used and is difficult to use accurately in a strictly legal context, it raises little doubt in the mind of the man in the street. Though definitional precision is difficult, terrorism is not hard to describe and, for those who have experienced it, easy to comprehend. "Terrorism is thus an easily recognized activity of a bad character, subjectively determined and shaped by social and political considerations."[3] The term is somewhat "Humpty Dumpty" -- anything we choose it to be. When the question "What is terrorism?" is raised, there are always present some sort of answers, though often colored by the purposes in asking it.[4]

From a purely physical perspective, terrorism is not easily isolable from wars, disasters, and accidents. This, combined with the known subjectivity of those who

seek to attach a definition to it, greatly complicates
any attempt to count and measure terrorist trends.[5]
Early attempts in the 1890s to isolate and deal with
terrorism spawned a number of theories. Cranial measures
of captured terrorists were taken. A connection between
terrorism and lunar phases was postulated. Cesare
Lombroso, a distinguished criminologist of his day, found
both a medical and a climatological explanation.
"Terrorism, like pellagra and some other diseases, was
caused by certain vitamin deficiencies, hence its pre-
valence among maize-eating people of Southern Europe."
He also found that the further north one went the less
terrorism there was.[6]

A serious attempt to define terrorism came in 1937
when the League of Nations formulated the Convention for
the Prevention and Punishment of Terrorism. The convention which was signed by twenty-four states, was
ratified by only one and never actually came into force.
It was a direct response to the assassination of King
Alexander I of Yugoslavia and the President of the
Council of the French Republic in 1934 by persons who
could be described as Yugoslav freedom fighters or
terrorists, depending upon one's political stance. The
drafters concerned themselves with the problem as they
saw it, namely preparation of a convention to prohibit
any form of planning or execution of terrorist outrages
upon the life or liberty of persons taking part in the
work of "foreign public authorities and services." The
convention was intended to suppress acts of terrorism
having an international character only. "Acts of
terrorism," as set forth in Article I, are "criminal
acts directed against a State and intended or calculated
to create a state of terror in the minds of particular
persons or the general public."[7]

It is interesting to note that the League's success-
or, the United Nations, has been unable to agree on a
definition of the term and has become diverted by an
"inconclusive" discussion of the causes and motives of
terrorists.[8]

With the exception of a number of bilateral agreements for the exchange of intelligence and technical
assistance, the international response to terrorism
continues to be relatively weak. The United Nations,
in the Declaration of Principles of International Law
Concerning Friendly Relations and Cooperation Among
States which the General Assembly adopted without vote
on October 24, 1970, asserts at one point that:

> Every State has the duty to refrain from
> organizing, instigating, assisting, or partic-
> ipating in acts of civil strife or terrorist
> acts in another state or acquiescing in organized

activity within its territory directed towards
the commission of such acts when the acts
referred to in the present paragraph involve
a threat or use of force.[9]

However, this same declaration clouds the issue by
the greater emphasis on "the principle of equal rights
and self-determination of peoples." The language employed in this regard implies that it is the overriding duty
of all states to assist groups struggling for the reali-
zation of these rights in every way possible. For example:

Every State has the duty to refrain from
any forcible action which deprives people above
in the elaboration of the present principles of
their right to self-determination and freedom
and independence. In their actions against, and
resistance to, such forcible action in pursuit
of the exercise of their right to self-determination, such peoples are entitled to seek and to
receive support in accordance with the purposes
and principles of the Charter.[10]

Despite the problems indicated above, international
conventions have dealt with certain aspects of the terrorism problem. These conventions are briefly summarized
below:

The Tokyo Convention (Convention on Offenses
and Certain Other Acts Committed on Board
Aircraft). Signed in September 1963, it did
not come into force until December 1969. It
is a very limited accord which does no more
than set a few jurisdictional ground rules
and requires the contracting states to: 1) make
every effort to restore control of the aircraft
to its lawful commander, and 2) arrange for the
prompt onward passage or return of hijacked
aircraft together with their passengers, cargo,
and crew.

The Montreal Convention (Convention for the
Suppression of Unlawful Acts Against the
Safety of Civil Aviation). Signed in September 1971, it came into force in January 1973.
Covering the sabotage or destruction of aircraft or air navigational facilities, it requires
the contracting parties to make such offenses
subject to severe penalties and establishes the
same extradition-or-prosecution system for offenders
as in The Hague Convention.

The Organization of American States Convention (Convention to Prevent and Punish Acts
of Terrorism Taking the Form of Crimes
Against Persons and Related Extortion that
are of International Significance). Signed
in February 1971, it entered into force in
October 1973 (the U.S. is a signatory, but
not a party). With its emphasis on the
prevention and punishment of crimes against
persons to whom the state owes a special
duty of protection under international law,
it was a precursor of the UN convention concerning the protection of diplomats which is
cited below. It also employs The Hague
Convention extradite-or-prosecute formula.

The United Nations Convention on the Prevention and Punishment of Crimes Against Internationally Protected Persons Including Diplomatic Agents. Signed in December 1973, it requires the contracting states to establish
certain specified acts against protected persons (or against the official premises, private
accommodations, or means of transport of such
a person) as crimes under international law.
Once again, The Hague Convention extradite-or-
prosecute formula applies.[11]

European Convention on the Suppression of
Terrorism. Signed and entered into force
August 4, 1978. It is very strong in its
wording and states that none of the many acts
(hijacking, kidnapping, use of bombs, grenades,
letter bombs, etc.) ".....shall be regarded as
a political offence or as an offence inspired
by political motives." While Austria, the
Federal Republic of Germany, and Sweden readily
signed; France, Italy, Norway, and Portugal
all attached reservations concerning the determination of a "political" offense.[12]

Convention Against Taking of Hostages. This
was debated by the U.N. during the first week
of December 1979 and gives the nations that
adhere to it a choice of prosecuting those who
seize others with the intention of forcing a
government to act or sending them back for
prosecution in their native land. The convention will come into force after twenty-two
nations sign it. One article was contested
by the Soviet Union and its East European
allies. This specifically provides for the

prosecution of a person who takes hostages
but spares him from being sent home if extra-
dition is requested to punish him for "race,
religion, nationality, ethnic origin or
political opinion." The Soviets offered a
counterproposal but it was defeated by a vote
of 103 to 10.[13]

Although the above conventions reflect some international concern, they do not constitute much of an
effective constraint on terrorist activity. Many states,
including a high percentage of those that have been particularly active in supporting revolutionary or national
liberation groups, are not yet parties thereto. Further,
the conventions lack teeth in that all make the extra-
dition or prosecution of terrorists subject to discre-
tionary escape clauses and none provide for the application of punitive sanctions against states that simply
refuse to comply at all.

Another aspect which makes defining terrorism difficult, other than the involvement of varying nationalities and cultures, is that it may be committed for
several purposes.[14] First, individual acts of terrorism
may aim at wringing specific concessions, such as the payment of ransom or release of prisoners. Second, terrorism may also attempt to gain publicity. Third, terrorism
may aim at causing widespread disorder, demoralizing
society and breaking down social order. Fourth, terrorism may target the deliberate provocation of repression,
hoping to induce the government to "self destruct."[15]
Fifth, terrorism may be used to enforce obedience and
cooperation. Sixth, terrorism is frequently meant to
punish. Terrorists often declare the victim of their
attack is somehow guilty.[16]

One fundamental aspect intimately related to the
term terrorism is that it is a bad word.[17] No one
desires to have the label applied to his activity.
Such terms as "freedom fighter" or "liberator" are
attempts to mitigate what is in fact an ugly profession.

To do unto others what is comprised in
terrorism is recognized everywhere as
being bad -- unless, like war, it can be
justified. Terrorism, so defined, is not
something that in all conscience can be
allowed of as being right and proper, unless there is a massive justification for
it -- in which case it is not terrorism![18]

Here we encounter the fine line between terror and
terrorism and the attempts to legalize or justify the
former while proscribing the latter. Terror practiced

by a government in office appears as law enforcement and is directed against the opposition. Terrorism, on the other hand, implies open defiance of law and is the means whereby an opposition aims to demoralize government authority. While the terrorist group makes no pretense at legality, legitimate government must at least formally adhere (or give the appearance of adhering) to the law. In the absence of directly supporting legislation, governmental terror is made to appear justified by declaring a state of emergency and the issuing of decrees.[19] From a legal point of view "there is nothing strange or incongruous about the dualism with which the phenomenon of terrorism is viewed."[20]

Another example worth noting relates to an identical set of physical facts, which can be criminal or noncriminal according to its association with a specific mental element. Murder and justifiable homicide are good examples. What is good or evil about the matter is not dependent upon the physical aspects of the case itself but rather the mind set that views it. "The true struggle over definition in the area of terrorism is fundamentally between those who claim an exception at law for certain manifestly harmful conduct and those who will not admit it."[21] When viewed this way, in terms of individual crimes, these acts, in and of themselves, are not terrorism. Terrorism is more the why of an act than the what.[22]

A definition of terrorism proposed by a lawyer familiar with international law is set forth below:[23]

> Terrorism involves the intentional use of violence or the threat of violence by the precipitator(s) against an instrumental target in order to communicate to a primary target a threat of future violence. The object is to use intense fear or anxiety to coerce the primary target to behavior or to mold its attitudes in connection with demanded power (political) outcome. It should be noted that in a specific context the instrumental and primary targets could well be the same person or group . . . . The crucial factor is that the task of deciding between the permissible and impermissible labels of a particular coercive process should be guided by community expectations and all relevant policies and features of context.

Terrorism, like beauty, remains in the eye of the beholder.[24]

Efforts expended in this book to reach an operational definition of terrorism are put forth not as an exercise in semantics but to illustrate the difficulty that

surrounds this particular term. Further, it is an attempt
to arrive at a readily workable definition that is more
than just one writer's view of this phenomenon. Studies
of terrorism must try, when possible, to develop more
precise language. Mutual use of commonly employed terms
is a prerequisite for expanding knowledge. With this
as a goal, the following definition is proffered:[25]

> Terrorism is a purposeful human political
> activity primarily directed toward the creation
> of a general climate of fear designed to influ-
> ence, in ways desired by the protagonist, other
> human beings and, through them, some course of
> events.

Terrorism poses an unacceptable challenge to the
principles on which an organized society rests. Those
acting in this way seek to arrogate to themselves the
use of powers normally reserved to the state. It is
expressed through the deliberate employment of various
criminal acts calculated to harm human life, property
or other interests.

Having presented an operational definition, it is
necessary to differentiate between types of terrorism.
The term international terrorism is frequently mentioned
in the literature. This should be clearly distinguished
from transnational terrorism. International terrorism
should be applied to groups or individuals controlled by
a sovereign state.[26] The term should not imply the existence of a "terrorist international"[27] in the sense of a
central body coordinating the activities of terrorists in
different countries. No evidence of such a body has been
discovered.[28]

Transnational terrorism is carried out by basically
autonomous nonstate actors, whether or not they enjoy
some degree of support from sympathetic states.[29] The
difficulty that surrounds accurate definition of terrorism
presents itself again in dealing with typologies.

Since the focus of this study is the countering of
transnational terrorism in the United States, the concern
is with the nature of the act as opposed to the nature of
the group. A transnational terrorist act may be viewed
as:

1. committed or taking effect outside the territory of a state of which the alleged offender
   is a national; and
2. committed or takes effect:
   a. outside the territory of the state against
      which the act is directed, or
   b. within the territory of the state against
      which the act is directed and the alleged

offender knows or has reason to know
that the instrumental target against
whom the act is directed is not a
national of that state;[30] or
c. the instrumental target is a national
of the primary target state but is a
different nationality than the state
of the offender; and
3. is intended to damage the interests of a
state or an international intergovernmental
organization;[31] and
4. is committed neither by nor against a member
of the armed forces of a state in the course
of military hostilities.

Before ending this chapter, two concepts should be
briefly addressed, namely nonterritorial terrorism and
domestic terrorism.

The term nonterritorial was coined when researchers
found other terminology lacking in the precision needed
to provide effective analysis. Nonterritorial terrorism
is defined as ". . . a form of terror not confined to a
clearly delineated geographical area."[32] Today's terrorist[33] is seen as having the potential of striking
virtually anywhere at will since, due to modern technology, he is not limited by space or geographical area.
While this definition removes barriers encountered in
trying to squeeze a group into either the international
or transnational definition, it, in a sense, removes all
barriers encompassing any group and is deemed too broad
for the purposes of this book.

Domestic terrorism concerns itself with activity
by a state's nationals in attempting to influence that
state's behavior. All activity would take place within
the geographical confines of that state.

Using these definitions as a basis, we will examine
in Chapter 7 how the concerned organizations of a government attempt to deal with countering the terrorist problem. We will explore this development as the pertinent
agencies, in seeking to define their jurisdictional responsibilities, interact in the national arena.

NOTES

1. Brian M. Jenkins, "International Terrorism:
A New Kind of Warfare," Report P-5216 (Santa Monica,
CA: Rand Corporation, June 1974), p. 1.

2. Ibid., pp. 3-4. To illustrate this, one has
only to recall the Symbionese Liberation Army. Through
the media everyone became familiar with the seven-headed
cobra symbol and heard audio tapes of the group's demands.

14

A significant number of FBI agents and police were mob-
ilized to track down the group. Patty Hearst's kidnapping added greatly to the notoriety as the group was
viewed nightly by millions on network news. However, it
was subsequently determined that the group had only a
dozen or so members at the height of its strength. At
its demise the group had committed one murder, one kidnapping, one bank job and a few stolen cars. The difference between actual violence and the amplified effects
of the violence is most significant. See also David
Anable, "Coming to Grips with World Terrorism," Christian Science Monitor, December 19, 1975, p. 3, where terrorism is described as the ". . . weapon of the weak . . .
whose shock waves then buffet millions."
        3. H.H.A. Cooper, "What is a Terrorist: A Psych-
ological Perspective," Legal Medical Quarterly, v. 1,
no. 1, 1977, p. 18, as reprinted in the U.S. Congress,
Senate, Committee on the Judiciary, The Terrorist and His
Victim, Hearings (Washington: U.S. Govt. Print. Off.,
1977).
        4. Ibid.
        5. Chalmers Johnson, "Perspectives on Terrorism,"
The Terrorism Reader, Walter Laqueur, ed. (New York:
A Meridian Book, New American Library, 1978), p. 269.
        6. Walter Laqueur, "Terrorism -- A Balance Sheet,"
The Terrorism Reader, pp. 262-263. Presumably Eskimos
would be immune from any inclinations in this direction.
        7. John Dugard, "International Terrorism: Prob-
lems of Definition," International Affairs (London),
v. 50, no. 1, January 1974, pp. 67-69.
        8. Louis Hoffacher, "The U.S. Government Response
to Terrorism," Vital Speeches of the Day, February 15,
1975, 41:266. While the speech is slightly dated, it
holds true today.
        9. United Nations, Yearbook of the United Nations:
1970 (New York: UN Office of Public Information, 1971),
p. 790.
        10. Ibid., p. 791.
        11. U.S. Central Intelligence Agency, International
and Transnational Terrorism: Diagnosis and Prognosis, by
David L. Milbank, Research Study PR 76 10030 (Washington,
DC: April 1976), p. 27.
        12. Yonah Alexander, et al., eds., Control of
Terrorism: International Documents (New York: Crane
Russak, 1979), pp. 87-109. This compilation contains the
text of treaties dating back to 1902 dealing with extra-
dition of those who commit terrorist or terrorist-like
acts. It also contains UN Resolutions and International
Civil Aviation Organization Resolutions.
        13. The New York Times, December 9, 1979, p. 12.

14. Brian M. Jenkins, "International Terrorism: A Balance Sheet," American Defense Policy, John E. Endicott and Roy W. Stafford, eds., Fourth Edition (Baltimore: Johns Hopkins University, 1977), pp. 184-186.

15. Brian Crozier, Director of the Institute for the Study of Conflict, London, in testimony before a U.S. Senate subcommittee indicated that there were two main categories of terrorism, disruptive and coercive. The aims of disruption are: self publicity; to build up the movement's morale and prestige; to discredit and demoralize the authorities; to provoke the authorities into taking excessively harsh repressive measures which are likely to alienate the population and force a rising spiral of official expenditures in arms, lives and money, resulting in public clamor for the abandonment of counter-eraction. On the other hand, the aims of coercive terrorism are: to demoralize the civil population, weaken its confidence in central authority and instill fear of the terrorist movement; to make an example of selected victims by torture and/or death to force obedience to the leadership of the movement. U.S. Congress, Senate, Committee on the Judiciary, Terrorist Activity - International Terrorism Hearings before a subcommittee of the Committee on the Judiciary, U.S. Senate, 94th Congress, 1st session, Part 4, 1974, p. 181.

16. Jenkins made this point most clearly with an illustration from the massacre at Lod Airport in 1972. He states that with terrorism there is a stronger connotation of guilt and punishment than in other forms of warfare or politics and a narrower definition of innocent bystanders. The victims of the Lod incident, many of whom were Christian pilgrims from Puerto Rico, were said by the terrorists to be guilty because they had arrived in Israel on Israeli visas and thereby had tacitly recognized the state that was the declared enemy of the Palestinians and, by coming to Israel, they had in effect entered a war zone. What was being said was not that the victims were innocent bystanders unfortunately caught in a crossfire; neither was the group saying that it would seek and kill all those holding visas from the State of Israel. The organization was saying that those who happened to get shot -- just because they were there -- were nonetheless guilty or they would not have been shot. Stated another way, they did not become victims because they were enemies but rather they became enemies because they happened to be victims. "A Balance Sheet," p. 186.

17. International Association of Chiefs of Police, Inc., Final Report, Needs Assessment Study: Terrorism in Dade County, Florida (Miami, FL: Dade-Miami Criminal Justice Council, July 1979), p. 10.

18. Ibid., p. 11. The governments of Mexico and Brazil have not frequently used the labels "terrorist" and "political" for the urban terrorists. They use instead "criminal" and "bandit," hoping to deprive the terrorists of any glamour. Such a tactic makes any system of repression easier to justify should the need arise. Albert Parry, Terrorism from Robespierre to Arafat (New York: Vanguard Press, Inc., 1976), p. 524.

19. J.B.S. Hardman, "Terrorism," The Encyclopedia of the Social Sciences, v. XIV (New York: Macmillan, 1964), p. 576.

20. International Association of Chiefs of Police, Inc., p. 12.

21. Ibid., p. 14.

22. One of the possible dangers that are embodied in the European Convention of 1978 cited above is its potential for not concerning itself with the why of a particular act. Blanket prohibition may be an overreaction and exemplify deterrence through overkill. The several attached reservations tend to endorse this view.

23. Jordan J. Paust, "A Survey of Possible Legal Responses to International Terrorism: Prevention, Punishment, and Cooperative Action," Georgia Journal of International and Comparative Law, vol. 5, 1975, pp. 434-435.

24. Numerous other definitions, or attempts at definition are found in many of the works cited in this chapter. Others of interest are Gaston Bouthoul, "Definitions of Terrorism," International Terrorism and World Security, David Carlton and Carlo Schaerf, eds., (New York: John Wiley and Sons, 1978), pp. 50-53; David Fromkin, "The Strategy of Terrorism," Foreign Affairs, vol. 53, July 1975, p. 690; Jan Schreiber, The Ultimate Weapon: Terrorists and World Order (New York: William Morrow and Co., Inc., 1978), pp. 20-37.

25. This definition closely resembles the one put forth on page 42 of the study by the International Association of Chiefs of Police, Inc. One of the major differences is the insertion of the word "political" between the words "human" and "activity." The reasons for doing this are to avoid admixing terrorism with gangland intimidation or similar acts. Terrorism is directly concerned with the exercise or the attempt to exercise public powers or influence the allocation of values by a ruling body. For those who may be interested in an excellently presented view of definitional efforts in this regard refer to the cited study.

26. U.S. Central Intelligence Agency, International and Transnational Terrorism, p. 9.

27. While this was stated by Brian Crozier as part of his testimony before the Senate subcommittee in 1975, all indications are that it is equally true today.

28. While a central authority may be missing there
are many indications of cooperation between groups and
open support from governments who support their objectives. A good example of this is the case of the Japanese
terrorists who carried out the Lod Airport attack. They
had received training in Syria and Lebanon; received
money passing through Germany; received their arms in
Italy and carried out their act for the Popular Front for
the Liberation of Palestine.

29. U.S. Central Intelligence Agency, _Interna-
tional and Transnational Terrorism_, p. 9. The author
makes the following point:

> Given the element of governmental patronage that
> is common to both, the boundary between trans-
> national and international terrorism is often
> difficult to draw. To the degree that it can
> be determined, the key distinction lies in who
> is calling the shots with respect to a given
> action or campaign. Hence, groups can and do
> drift back and forth across the line. For ex-
> ample, even a one time "contract job" undertaken
> on behalf of a governmental actor by a group
> that normally acts according to its own rights
> qualifies as international terrorism.

30. The person or persons against whom the act is
directed may be either the primary or instrumental target
as was indicated previously.

31. Dugard, p. 79. The basis of this definition
was taken from Article 1 of the Draft Convention for Prevention and Punishment of Certain Acts of International
Terrorism, submitted by the United States to the United
Nations General Assembly, September 26, 1972. For a complete text see Alexander, et al, eds., _Control of Terror-
ism_, pp. 113-118. If we were to concern ourselves with
the particular groups we would seek to examine not only
the site of the act but also such relevant aspects as
the nationalities or foreign ties (i.e., training, funding, arms) of the group, sanctuaries, declared ideology
and mechanics of the act's resolution.

32. Stephen Sloan and Richard Kearney, "Non-
Territorial Terrorism: An Empirical Approach to Policy
Formulation," _Conflict_, Vol. I, No. 1 and 2, 1978,
p. 132. See also Sloan, _The Anatomy of Non-Territorial
Terrorism, An Analytical Essay_, International Association
of Chiefs of Police, Inc., 1978 (Gaithersburg, MD) IACP.
Brian Jenkins makes reference to this same phenomena when
he describes terrorism as: "It is a warfare without territory, waged without armies as we know them. It is warfare that is not limited territorially; sporadic 'battles'

may take place worldwide.   It is warfare without neutrals, and with few or no civilian bystanders."   "A New Kind of Warfare," p. 4.

33. The prolonged situation in Iran can be viewed (based upon available evidence) as initially beginning as mob action directed against the United States.   However, as the incident progressed and governmental sanction of the activity was given, the act took on the flavor of international terrorism.   In this sense the Iranian case can be viewed as evolving into a terrorist act since the initial "purposefulness" is a matter of speculation.

3
The Organizational Perspective

Modern man is man in organizations.[1]

Give me the patience to accept what cannot be
changed in the organization, the courage to
change what can be changed, and the wisdom to
know the difference.[2]

It is fundamental to this study that organizations,
in and of themselves, are important. People spend a
great portion of their time in organizations. The bulk
of the adult population -- the working force -- spends
at least one-third of its life in some form of organization. Children, upon entry into school, are affected
by and participate in organizations. Mail orders are
processed, patients in hospitals tended to, traffic fines
paid, milk delivered, autos repaired, prisoners executed, priests ordained, laws passed and much, much more
accomplished in an organizational environment. Since
organizations impinge on so many aspects of our society,
elements of organizational theory can be drawn together
from various sources: (1) executives have recorded
their experiences in biographical form in books or articles;[3] (2) the scientific management movement has
concerned itself with organizational theory, and most
works devote chapters to statements of principles of
good organization;[4] (3) sociologists (especially noted
are Max Weber and Talcott Parsons) have delved deeply
into organization theory;[5] (4) psychologists have
studied leadership, supervision and morale within organizations;[6] and (5) political scientists have been concerned about the efficient operations of governmental
organizations and democratic control over governmental
administration.[7] Despite the volume of writings, one
is left with the impression that "after all, not a great
deal has been said about organizations, but it has been
said over and over in a variety of languages."[8]
    This book centers on the effects organizational
processes have had upon the development of a policy to

19

counter terrorism. Governmental action in this regard
will be examined from the time of President Richard
Nixon's 1972 statement creating the Committee to Combat
Terrorism through the beginning of the Reagan administration. During this period organizations within the federal
government were directed to develop (or independently
sought to become part of) a viable counterterror program.
The success or failure of such endeavors is a subjective
judgement. What is clear, however, is that organizations
came face to face with a phenomenon (an environment)
which caused them to modify procedures or structures.
Additionally, some organizations attempted to alter the
environment which allowed terrorist acts to be carried
out. The subjectivity results from the perspective by
which success or failure is measured -- Did the organization adapt successfully to the environment? Did such
an adaptation result in maintaining the health of the
organization, solving the problem, or both?

Organizations can be termed social inventions
or tools developed by men to accomplish what otherwise
would be unattainable. They are usually composed of
people, knowledge, and material in some structured fashion. Separate parts become an integrated whole. Once
it exists, people are aware of an organization and those
in it look at each other not just as individuals but
for what they contribute to the organized effort of
which they are part. Although composed of individuals,
organizations take on an identity of their own.[9]

Organizations come into existence when explicit procedures are established to coordinate the activities of
a group in the interest of achieving specified objectives.
It may be argued that whenever groups of individuals
associate with one another, social organization develops.
In this research we are going beyond such groupings, to
what will be termed formal organizations. The defining
criterion then becomes the existence of procedures for
the mobilization and coordination of efforts of various,
usually specialized, subgroups in the pursuit of objectives.[10]

What makes the study of organizations particularly
interesting is that actual interaction and activity
within them never corresponds precisely to official
prescriptions and design. Further, it is often difficult
to determine the boundaries of an organization, to know
definitely where one organization begins and another ends.
It is not unusual for someone or a group from outside a
particular organization to be able to influence what
goes on within an organization. In the private sector,
creditors and/or investors may well have great importance in determining how an organization will run even
though they do not appear on any organizational chart.[11]
In the public sector, the influence of Congressional

budget committees upon Department of Defense spending can be quite profound. Yet no study of the Department of Defense in and of itself would develop this information.[12]

The concern with organizations is relevant to the study of our governmental response to transnational terrorism. This is based upon the fact that governments perceive problems through organizational sensors. Alternatives are defined and consequences estimated as governmental organizations process information. Governments act as their organizations enact routines. In efforts to be responsive to the wide spectrum of problems confronted every day, governments consist of large organizations among which primary responsibility for particular tasks is divided. Government behavior thus reflects the independent output of several organizations, partially coordinated by leaders who can "substantially disturb but not substantially control the behavior of these organizations."[13]

One of the earliest attempts to come to grips with the impact of organizations on society was conducted by the German sociologist, Max Weber. Weber asserted that one of the major features of modern society was the presence of large multifaceted organizations. He saw emerging an industrial society functioning within a regulated impersonal framework where hierarchy and specialization would be dominating characteristics. These "bureaucratic" aspects were principally as follows:

1. Organization tasks are distributed among various positions as official duties. Implied in this is a clear-cut division of labor among positions which make possible a high degree of specialization. Specialization, in turn, promotes expertness among the staff.
2. Positions or offices are organized into hierarchical authority structures.
3. A formally established system of rules governs official decisions and actions. This insures a uniformity of operations and a continuity of operations regardless of changes in personnel.
4. Officials are expected to assume an impersonal orientation which is designed to prevent the personal feelings of officials from distorting their rational judgement.
5. Employment by the organization constitutes a career during which officials are appointed, becoming dependent on their superiors.[14]

Weber emphasized that the foundation of legitimate social order is a common value orientation that effects social control and compliance with authoritative commands.

The authority structure is the core of any organization.[15]
    Building upon the foundation laid by Weber, advo-
cates of the scientific theory sought to discover the
most effective methods of organizing to accomplish set
goals. These studies were mechanistic and prescriptive
in nature as they sought to learn the one best way to
get the job done, often employing time-motion studies
as an analyzing tool.[16]
    Based upon Weber's concern with organizational struc-
ture another approach to the study of organizations developed in the 1920s. This school, employing what would
come to be known as classical administrative theory,
sought to develop better ways to delegate, coordinate,
and specialize. Workers were to be grouped according to
purpose, methods, or location, and their number per super-
visor was to be limited, insuring an adequate span of
control. One of the dangers of the classical administrative approach is that there is a tendency for vast
hierarchies to develop. These hierarchies, in turn,
become dysfunctional as they seek to deal with the processing of information, react to the environment, and
come to grips with internal conflict. "The vagueness
of these early approaches to organizing accounts for
much of the confusion in the field today."[17] A good
example of the vagueness can be seen in the debate between proponents of various theories relative to organizational goals.

    Classical administrative theorists must have
    a set of goals for the organization because
    without it, they cannot prescribe the approp-
    riate organizing principles. Human relations
    and scientific management theorists must also
    have a set of goals for the same prescriptive
    purpose. In each of the early approaches, the-
    orists assumed that organizations had a goal
    or set of goals that were widely shared and
    understood by the members of that organization
    - an assumption that leads one to describe
    large, complex organizations as if they were
    a cohesive unit. In fact, the members of the
    same bureaucracy may have different goals.[18]

    In any discussion of organizations, time and space
is devoted to analyzing organizational goals. This is
no easy task since almost any sequence of behavior can
be cut into small or large pieces, each of which can
be said to be goal-directed. What is designated as a
goal as well as what is used as evidence for the existence of a goal may be closely related to the focus of
the study itself.

In the process of decision, those alternatives are chosen which are considered to be appropriate means for achieving desired ends. Yet, these ends may of themselves be instruments for reaching more final objectives. "We are thus led to the conception of a series, or hierarchy, of ends."[19] The fact that goals may be dependent for their force on other, more distant ends, leads to this structuring with each level considered as an end relative to the levels below it and a means relative to the levels above it. This hopefully leads to an integration and consistency of action.

While this is the ideal, Herbert A. Simon argues that a high degree of conscious integration is seldom attained. Often the connection between organizational activities and ultimate objectives is obscure, or the ultimate objectives are incompletely formulated, or there are internal conflicts and contradictions among the ultimate objectives or among the means to attain them. For example, conflictual opinions come to the fore when discussing the extent to which an agency such as the FBI can go in protecting society in general while infringing upon the freedoms (speech, assembly) of a small group. What would be the goal when terrorists seize a foreign ambassador from a volatile nation and hold him hostage on a U.S. airliner? Would we mainly be concerned with the lives of the hostages and other passengers? Would we mainly be concerned with the safety of victims and the apprehension of the group? Would we be more concerned with possible retribution against U.S. citizens residing in the volatile nation? Representatives of the FBI, Department of State, and the airlines may well have differing answers to each question.

It is a safe assumption that not all organizational goals lead to some single ultimate end. Rather, organizations pursue a variety of goals and some may be in competition with one another. Nor do goals stay constant. Often a succession of goals takes place which involves changes in output characteristics rather than in categories of outputs. An example relating to a general hospital disclosed that, as control of the organization passed from trustees to doctors and then from doctors to administrators, the characteristics of product goals also changed, together with investor goals and derived goals. There was a shift from emphasis on serving indigent Jews to one serving middle-class Jews and Gentiles, an increase in research as opposed to teaching and the development of programs that competed with non-Jewish hospitals, whereas previously such programs had been avoided.[20]

Public organizations such as the FBI have undergone similar changes throughout their history. Most recently the traditional apprehension of military deserters and investigations of bank robberies have passed to other

agencies, both federal and local. One of the driving
reasons behind these changes is that such cases were not
economical. However, cases involving white-collar crime
and fraud in such programs as Medicaid were costing the
government millions of dollars and the investigative resources available were minimal. Thus, the FBI found
itself changing the characteristics of its output when
compared to the past.[21]

One danger that exists in the pursuit of goals is a
phenomenon of goal displacement. This entails the adher-
ence to the prescribed means which interferes with the
achievement of the goals themselves. The emphasis on
the way goals are to be reached leads to a transference
of the sentiments from the aims of the organization onto
the particular details of behavior required by the rules.
The practice of adhering to the rules, originally conceived
as a means, becomes an end in itself. Thus, "an instrumental value becomes a terminal value."[22] This emphasis
develops into rigidity and an inability to adjust readily
-- exaggeration to the point where concern with conformity
to the rules interferes with the achievement of the purposes of the organization.

A good example of this phenomenon was demonstrated
in the organizing of the Joint Task Force to free the
hostages in Iran, November 1979 through April 1980. In
a report issued on August 24, 1980 by Admiral (Ret.)
James L. Holloway, III, who headed the panel to analyze
the mission, it was clearly stated that the "seemingly
non-discriminating over-emphasis" on secrecy comprised
the mission from the beginning. All other issues, to
include the ultimate goal of freeing the hostages,
somehow became subordinate to what should have been one
aspect among many: i.e., clear lines of command, adequate
coordinated training, intelligence gathering, etc. In
each of the problem areas surrounding the mission, the
review group was able to name an alternative course,
which it concluded "would have had no effect or only a
minimal one on security while substantially - if not
critically - improving the chances of success."[23]

While earlier studies of organizations centered more
on structure, current approaches have dealt more with the
way organizations behave. Decisions and how they are
formulated and carried out have been the focus of one
school. It is noted that the decisions made by men in
organizations are quite different from rational decisions. There are, in fact, numerous obstacles to ration-
ality that inhibit an individual's ability to process,
store and retrieve data. Additionally, pressures often
exist which demand a decision be made in a limited time-
frame without the opportunity to examine all the consequences. The decision process tends to be characterized
by the following:

1. Optimizing is replaced with "satisficing" --
   the requirement that satisfactory or acceptable
   levels of criterion variables be attained.
2. Alternatives of action and consequences of
   action are discovered sequentially through a
   search process.
3. Repertoires of action programs are developed
   by organizations which serve as alternatives of
   choice in recurrent situations.
4. Each specific action program deals with a
   restricted range of situations and a restricted
   range of consequences. Action programs are
   capable of being executed in semi-independent
   ways only loosely connected.

The one-thing-at-a-time approach is fundamental to
the very existence of what is termed organization structure. Organizational structure consists of those aspects
of the pattern of behavior in the organization that are
relatively stable and that change only slowly. At any
given time an organization's programs for performing its
tasks are part of its structure.[25]
Graham T. Allison has expanded upon the characteristics described above and developed additional aspects relevant to organizational theory. One aspect is the factoring of problems which are seen as so complex that only a
limited number of items can be attended to at any time.
Thus problems are factored in quasi-independent parts
one by one. Organizations factor complex problems into
a number of roughly independent parts which are parceled
out to various organizational units. The structure of an
organization in turn reflects the problems that its subunits factor.[26] What we shall encounter as this book
develops is that several organizations have been faced
with the task of countering terrorism. Accordingly, parts
of these organizations' structure reflect the problem as
factored by their subunits. This factoring process developed relatively independently in each organization and,
consequently, presents problems as jurisdictional and
bureaucratic interests converge. While factored problems
and the accompanying fractionized power permit more
specialized attention, they also encourage organizational
parochialism.[27]
Closely related to this is an organization's tendency to vest and weigh particular interests and perspectives.[28] Organizational arrangements -- that is, the
existence of specific departments, the distribution of
powers among them, and procedures for communication --
determine whether and how effectively particular considerations will be represented. A central question in organizational design is which substantive perspectives
should be introduced, with what weights given in the

processes of decision and action. An interest can be
vested in several ways but most vividly, in our case, by
the creation of a specific agency expressly dedicated to
countering terrorism. Interests can also be vested by
establishing units within existing organizations (for
example, the Office to Combat Terrorism in the Department
of State). Giving weight to an interest is another matter.
Weight can be equated with power. It could come about
from formal authority, from control of resources or from
special competence. Weight does not follow, however, as
a matter of course from vesting[29] as will be clearly
evident when we examine the Office to Combat Terrorism
in the Department of State.

The reliable performance of a task requires standard
operating procedures (SOPs). These rules permit standard
action by large numbers of individuals responding to basic
cues. The rules are generally simple enough to facilitate
easy learning. Since the procedures are "standard," they
do not change easily or quickly. Further, because of SOPs,
organizational behavior in particular instances appears
formalized and sometimes inappropriate.[30]

Organizations, furthermore, must be able to conduct
actions in which the behavior of hundreds of individuals
is closely coordinated. Assured performance requires sets
of SOPs for producing specific actions. These sets com-
prise a program that the organization has available for
dealing with a situation. The list of programs constitutes an organizational repertoire. The number of programs in a repertoire is always limited and cannot be
changed in substance in a particular situation.[31]

Two interesting examples of organizational inability
to act without SOPs and programs recently showed themselves.
Despite the growing concern for environmental hazards due
to improper disposal of chemicals, very few cases have
been initiated against major chemical companies. A prime
reason centers on the Environmental Protection Agency itself. Even though the Resource Conservation and Recovery
Act was passed in 1976, the Agency has yet (1980) to
issue the needed regulations (i.e., SOPs) to give full
force to the Act. In the meantime, the Justice Department, according to then Attorney General Benjamin R.
Civiletti, had created a new unit to handle prosecutions
involving hazardous wastes. He felt that he could not
wait for the EPA to act and would take action under the
one clearly defined authorization of the 1976 Act, i.e.,
"imminent hazard." Any prosecutorial action relating to
more long-term hazards will still have to wait for the
EPA to issue the needed regulations.[32]

A second example showed itself during the Iranian
rescue mission. The Holloway Report took issue with the
ad hoc nature of the organization and planning of the mission. "By not utilizing an existing JTF (Joint Task Force)

organization, the Joint Chiefs of Staff (JCS) had to start, literally, from the beginning to establish a JTF, create an organization, provide a staff, develop a plan, select the units, and train the force...."[33] Existing contingency plans (CONPLAN) were not employed, and while the particular circumstances surrounding the Iranian mission may have differed, established programs would have provided the "conceptual basis for an additional capability."[34] The Holloway group's evaluation made it quite clear that the "application of an existing JCS CONPLAN and JCS/Service doctrinal precepts could have improved the organization, planning, and preparation of the force through unity of command and cohesion of effort. That, in turn, would have led to more effective command and control and enhanced overall JTF readiness."[35]

It is theorized that organizations seek to avoid uncertainty. It is highly desirable to be able to estimate the probabilities of outcomes. Decision makers are reluctant to base actions on estimates of an uncertain future. By arranging a negotiated environment, organizations regularize the reaction of other actors with whom they have to deal. The primary environment (i.e., relations with other organizations within the government) is stabilized by such arrangements as agreed budget splits, accepted areas of responsibility, and established practices. (This is not always easily or readily achieved, especially when the essence/role of an organization is threatened.) When dealing with terrorists the opportunity for such stabilization does not present itself. Uncertainty tends to remain just that. To cope as best they can, governmental organizations will develop a set of scenarios that constitute contingencies for which they prepare.[36]

The style of the search for a contingency plan and its stopping point is largely determined by existing routines. The neighborhood of the symptom is searched first, then the neighborhood of the current alternative. (Tactics for handling hostage cases with terrorists were not developed anew. Rather, techniques learned from previous cases, i.e., kidnapping, were expanded upon to meet the new situations.) Patterns of search reveal organizational biases that reflect such factors as specialized training and experience.[37]

It has been argued that, despite what may be stated publicly as to what an organization's goals really are, most define the central goal as being "healthy." By this is meant growth in budgets, manpower, and territory. Where boundaries are ambiguous and changing, actions are dominated by "colonizing activity."[38]

Sometimes this activity as well as shifts in organizational behavior can be the result of action by government leaders. While it was indicated previously that these leaders, as they sit atop the conglomerate of

organizations, have limited ability to control changes,
especially in particular organizations' goals or SOPs,
many important issues of government action require that
these leaders decide what organizations will enact what
programs. Thus important shifts in the behavior of government can take place with little change in a particular
organization's parochialism. The leaders' options for
shifting governmental behavior include: (1) triggering
program A rather than B; (2) triggering existing organizational routines in a new context; and (3) triggering
several different organizations' programs simultaneously.[39]

Such actions by government leaders could well be
a cause of interagency rivalry and detract from the effectiveness of any action. Rivalry, in and of itself,
is not confined to the interorganizational realm but is
also located within organizations. The term organization does suggest a certain bareness exemplified by a
system of consciously coordinated activity. Yet, such
a formal design never completely accounts for what the
participants do. Formal procedures may coordinate roles
or specialized activity, but not people. "The formal,
technical system is therefore never more than a part of
the living enterprise we deal with in action."[40] The
relations outlined on an organizational chart provide a
framework within which fuller human behavior takes place.

Approaches to the study of organizations set forth
in this chapter all assume that organizational activity
is planned and purposeful - "the underlying assumption
is that people know what they are doing."[41] Yet situations exist where there is constant change, with several
participants entering the process at different times,
attempting to define a complex situation where values and
decision making variables make analyses most difficult.
The result is more a form of organized anarchy where the
activity is described afterwards in a fashion that appears
rather systematic. The size and scope of today's national
bureaucracies resemble mega-organizations which are in-
fluenced by several factors:

1. A lack of consensus about just what one should
   be doing at a particular point in time. Should
   the U.S. counterterror effort center on deterrence?
   While an incident is underway does the safety of
   the hostages override all other considerations?
   Is terrorism a criminal or a political phenomenon?
2. A lack of a clear delineation of authority and
   full understanding of how an organization or a
   group of organizations function. While it is
   acknowledged the president has the option of
   running the show in any counterterror effort,
   will he in fact exercise that option? If he does,
   will he choose to employ existing programs and
   groups or create new ones?

3. The fact is that issues (such as a terrorist
   attack) appear from out of the blue, leaving
   little time for careful deliberation and long
   term analysis. Additionally, issues do not
   arise one at a time but rather as one among
   several, further taxing the decision maker
   and organization.
4. The external environment with which organizations must deal is often more murky than clear.
   As indicated in the previous chapter, terrorism
   can be undertaken for various purposes. The
   target may be government or private -- or a
   combination of the two. The site of the attack
   may be singular or a series of locations, i.e.,
   multiple hijackings.

As we examine the governmental structure to combat
terrorism the various approaches to the study of organizations must be reviewed and reflected upon. Out of this
body of thought we will attempt to draw out the relevant
principles which help explain the nature of the U.S.
response as it evolved from 1972. We begin our journey
in the next chapter.

NOTES

1. Peter Blau and W. Richard Scott, Formal Organizations, A Comparative Approach (San Francisco, CA: Chandler
Publishing Company, 1962), p. ix.
2. David R. Hampton, Charles E. Summer and Ross A.
Webber, Organizational Behavior and the Practice of
Management (IL: Scot, Foresman and Company, 1968),
p. 185.
3. For an interesting contrast between experience
in private and business organizations see W. Michael Blumenthal, "Candid Reflections of a Businessman in Washington," Fortune, January 29, 1979, pp. 36-48.
4. See Robert N. Anthony and Regina Herzlinger,
Management Control in Nonprofit Organizations (Homewood,
IL: Richard D. Irwin, Inc., 1975); David J. Lawless,
Organization Behavior (Englewood Cliffs, NJ: Prentice-
Hall, Inc., 1979); and L.L. Cummings and W.E. Scott, Jr.,
eds., Readings in Organizational Behavior and Human Performance (Homewood, IL: Richard D. Irwin, Inc., 1969).
5. Talcott Parsons, Structure and Process in Modern Societies (Glencoe, IL: Free Press, 1960).
6. Irving L. Janis, Victims of Groupthink (Boston,
MA: Houghton Mifflin, 1972).
7. Harold L. Wilensky, Organizational Intelligence
(New York: Basic Books, 1967).

8. James G. March and Herbert A. Simon, _Organiza-tions_ (New York, London & Sydney: John Wiley & Sons, Inc., 1958), pp. 3-5.

9. Joseph A. Litterer, _Analysis of Organizations,_ 2nd ed. (New York, London & Sydney: John Wiley & Sons, Inc., 1973), p. 5.

10. Peter Blau, "Organizations," _International Encyclopedia of Social Science,_ v. 11 (New York: Mac-millan, 1968), p. 298.

11. Litterer, pp. 6-7.

12. Lawrence J. Korb, "An Analysis of the Con-gressional Budget Act of 1974," _Naval War College Review,_ Spring 1977, pp. 40-52.

13. Graham T. Allison, _Essence of Decision_ (Bos-ton, MA: Little, Brown & Co., 1971), pp. 69-71.

14. H.H. Gerth and C. Wright Mills, eds.,_From Max Weber: Essays in Sociology_ (New York: Oxford Uni-versity Press, 1946), pp. 196-204.

15. Max Weber, _The Theory of Social and Economic Organization,_ A. M. Henderson and Talcott Parsons, trans. (Glencoe, IL: Free Press and Falcon's Wing Press, 1947), p. 152.

16. Frederick W. Taylor, _The Principles of Scien-tific Management_ (New York: Harper Bros., 1911).

17. James C. Thompson, _Rolling Thunder_ (Chapel Hill, NC: University of North Carolina Press, 1980), p. 107.

18. _Ibid._, pp. 108-109.

19. Herbert A. Simon, _Administrative Behavior_ (New York: The Free Press, 1976), pp. 62-66. See also Talcott Parsons, _Structure of Social Action_ (New York: The Free Press, 1968), pp. 44, 49. Parsons sees an end, "in the analytical sense," as being defined as the _dif-ference_ between the anticipated future state of affairs and that which it could have been predicted would ensue from the initial situation _without the agency of the actor having intervened._

20. Charles Perrow, "Hospitals: Technology, Structure and Goals," in James March, ed., _Handbook of Organizations_ (Chicago, IL: Rand McNally, 1965), pp. 947-951.

21. Interview with Special Agent Thomas Love, Federal Bureau of Investigation, Ann Arbor Office, Ann Arbor, Michigan, July 1979.

22. Robert K. Merton, _Social Theory and Social Structure_ (New York: The Free Press, 1957), pp. 195-199.

23. _The Washington Post_, Editorial, "Desert One Revisited," Sunday, August 31, 1980, p. D6. This opinion is shared by the author, who has read the Holloway Report in its entirety.

24. March and Simon, p. 169.

25. _Ibid._, pp. 169-171.

26. Allison, p. 72.

27. Ibid., p. 8. Another danger of factoring is the excessive division of labor within an organization. A recent study by the West German Defense Ministry of their army disclosed that it was "increasingly bureaucratic, lacking soul and divorced from the soldiers in its ranks." The armed forces were functionally and technically efficient but had become cooler and, at times, even cold in their functions. The report concluded that the 495,000 members of the armed forces had too many tasks to fulfill, resulting in selective obedience, lower quality performance, and neglect of some duties. This has resulted in an over-emphasis on technical proficiency and centralization which has hurt creativity and motivation. The New York Times, November 4, 1979, p. 8.

28. Graham Allison and Peter Stanton, Remaking Foreign Policy: The Organizational Connection (New York: Basic Books, Inc., 1976), pp. 21-22.

29. The Arms Control and Disarmament Agency was created in 1961 (vested) for the purpose of giving institutional voice to that serious problem. Recent history has shown that the weight possessed by the Agency is not all that substantial with the President, State, and DOD all participating/controlling to some degree.

30. Allison, p. 83.

31. Ibid., Simon and March, p. 150.

32. New York Times, November 4, 1979, p. 25.

33. James L. Holloway, III, et al, "Rescue Mission Report," Unpublished paper dated August 1980, p. vi.

34. Ibid., p. 17.

35. Ibid., p. 18.

36. Allison, pp. 72, 84. Most large law enforcement agencies have developed scenarios to handle hostage situations. Yet techniques will vary among agencies and differences in negotiation styles emerge. How long should one negotiate? What role should he assume? More directly relevant to the organizational approach of this study is: Which representative of which agency should negotiate in the first place?

37. Ibid., p. 85.

38. Allison, p. 93.

39. Ibid., p. 87.

40. Philip Selznick, Leadership in Administration (New York: Harper and Row, 1957), p. 8.

41. Thompson, p. 129. What follows is a summary of the organized anarchy theory or the so-called "garbage can theory" as set forth in pages 129-134.

4
Governmental Structure to Counter Terrorism

With the stunning massacre at Lod Airport and the brutal slayings during the Olympics at Munich in 1972, terrorism, with all its ramifications, became more apparent throughout the world. While the U.S. had been relatively free of this type of violence, it appeared that some type of federal response was needed -- if only to deter terrorist groups from carrying out activity on American soil.

On September 22, 1972, President Richard M. Nixon sent a memorandum to the Secretary of State, William Rogers, establishing the Cabinet Committee to Combat Terrorism. The Committee was to be chaired by the Secretary of State and comprised of the Secretary of the Treasury, the Secretary of Defense, the Attorney General, the Secretary of Transportation, the United States Ambassador to the U.N., the Director of the Central Intelligence Agency, the Assistant to the President for Domestic Affairs, the Director of the Federal Bureau of Investigation, and such others as the chairman might consider necessary. The Cabinet Committee was to be supported by a Working Group comprised of personally designated senior representatives of members of the Committee and chaired by the designee of the Secretary of State.[1]

Federal officers and federal departments and agencies were "to cooperate fully with the Cabinet Committee in carrying out its functions under this directive, and they shall comply with the policies, guidelines, standards, and procedures prescribed by the Cabinet Committee."[2]

More specifically, the Committee was to:

1. Coordinate, among the government agencies, ongoing activity for the prevention of terrorism. This will include such activities as the collection of intelligence world wide and the physical protection of U.S. personnel and installations abroad and foreign diplomats and diplomatic installations in the United States.

2. Evaluate all such programs and activities and where necessary recommend methods for their effective implementation.
3. Devise procedures for reacting swiftly and effectively to acts of terrorism that occur.
4. Make recommendations to the Director of the Office of Management and Budget concerning proposed funding of such programs, and;
5. Report to the President, from time to time, concerning the foregoing.[3]

The first meeting of the Cabinet Committee was held on October 2, 1972. The Committee agreed that the initiatives already taken to attack the problem of terrorism were realistic ways to respond to the widespread threat.[4] In addition, it was also decided that new initiatives should be made to the International Civil Aviation Organization; increased efforts to share intelligence among nations should be fostered; the U.N. ambassador should push for the adoption of a draft convention to hinder terrorist activity; and lastly, the Working Group was to begin immediately to develop contingency plans in anticipation of terrorist acts. Armin H. Meyer, the former U.S. Ambassador to Japan, was nominated and approved as State's Special Assistant and Coordinator to Combat Terrorism.[5]

From the perspective of overall policy, the "preventive aspect of our mandate" was emphasized.[6] Initial efforts were aimed at improving procedures in the U.S. and abroad to detect and deter the terrorists. U.S. government policy guidelines for dealing with terrorism in the United States having international aspects or implications contained eleven steps.[7]

1. The U.S. Government seeks to maintain firm, effective, and consistent antiterrorist policies at home and abroad.
2. We seek to exert leadership, by example and by diplomacy, in attempting to find collective solutions to this international problem.
3. The U.S. Government is committed to pursue legal remedies in dealing with terrorists and endeavors to influence other governments to do likewise.
4. Under principles of customary international law, the host government of a country where an act of terrorism occurs is responsible for providing protection to foreign nationals within its territory, including securing their safe release from captors.

5. Accordingly, in an incident in the U.S. involving foreign nationals, the U.S. Government undertakes negotiations to secure the release of hostages. The FBI, under guidance from the Attorney General, has clear responsibilities in this effort, in collaboration with other law enforcement agencies. The Department of State exercises responsibilities in any aspects touching on relations with other governments.

6. The U.S. Government does not pay ransom, release prisoners or otherwise yield to blackmail by terrorists' groups.

7. We establish effective communication with terrorists whose hostages are under U.S. protective responsibilities, avoiding hard and fast positions, except as noted above, while seeking to reduce, or ideally to terminate, danger to hostages.

8. The U.S. Government generally opposes but cannot prevent foreign governments, private individuals, or companies from meeting terrorists' demands, including payment of ransom.

9. The U.S. Government adheres to the principle that a terrorist should be prosecuted for criminally defined acts of terrorism within the country of commission or be extradited to a country having appropriate jurisdiction to try the offender.

10. While political motivations such as the achievement of self-determination or independence are cited by some individuals or groups to justify terrorism, the U.S. rejects terrorism in any circumstances. Political objectives should be addressed in appropriate forums rather than by resort to violence against innocent bystanders.

11. The U.S. Government seeks the reduction or elimination of the causes of terrorism at home and abroad, including legitimate grievances which might motivate potential terrorists.

Additionally, policy was set forth concerning incidents abroad. However, as time passed, all these guidelines were modified and a single list of seven items was promulgated, stressing the condemnation of terrorism, international cooperation, and refusal to meet the terrorist demands.[8]

The antiterrorist program as developed during President Jimmy Carter's administration comprised four basic program components:[9]

1. Prevention. International initiatives and diplomacy to discourage state support of terrorism and to build a broad consensus

that terrorist acts are inadmissible under
international law irrespective of the cause
in which they are used.

2. Deterrence. Protection and security efforts
   of the public and private sectors to discourage
   terrorists acts -- essentially target hardening.
3. Reaction. Antiterrorism operations in response
   to specific major acts of terrorism.
4. Prediction. Intelligence and counterintelligence
   efforts in continuous support of the other three
   program components.[10]

Because of the inactivity of the Cabinet Committee,
the Carter administration decided to formulate a more
responsive policy to the threat of terrorism. The original committee was abolished in late 1977. Pursuant to
Presidential Review Memorandum (PRM) No. 30, the federal
government's response to domestic and international terrorism was reorganized under the aegis of the Special Coordination Committee (SCC) of the National Security Council (NSC). The NSC is the principal forum for international security issues requiring presidential consideration. Its purpose is to assist the president in "analyzing, integrating, and facilitating foreign, defense, and
intelligence policy decisions. International economic
and other interdependence issues which are pertinent to
national security are also considered by the NSC."[11]

Not only did President Carter revise the way the NSC
handled terrorism, but he also revised the way the NSC
itself functioned. He established[12] two major policy
organs, the Policy Review Committee (PRC) and the SCC.
The PRC, whose chairman rotated according to the subject
under review and whose membership was the same as the
Council's, worked on long-term projects. The SCC, whose
chairman was always the Assistant to the President for
National Security Affairs and whose membership duplicated
that of the Council, focused on short-term projects. Both
the PRC and the SCC had their own working group. Depending upon the project, these working groups were composed of
officials at either the undersecretary or assistant secretary level.

As indicated by Ambassador Anthony Quainton, director of the State Department's Office for Combating Terrorism:[13]

In practice, the SCC would probably directly
exercise this responsibility only in the event
of a major terrorist incident requiring highest
level decisions. In general, the U.S. Government's response to terrorist incidents is based
on the lead agency concept: the State Department has operational responsibility for international incidents; the Department of Justice

and FBI handle domestic incidents coming under
Federal jurisdiction. They work closely with
state and local law enforcement authorities
where there is overlapping jurisdiction. Aircraft hijacking is a special case -- the Congress
has mandated by law that the Federal Aviation
Administration shall have primary responsibility
in this field. Each of these agencies can and
does draw upon the support of other Federal
agencies with relevant expertise. Where interagency policy issues arise during the course of
an incident, senior officials of concerned agencies can meet, under NSC staff leadership, to
resolve them.

The senior-level interagency Executive Committee
on Terrorism (ECT), which consisted of representatives
from the departments of State, Defense, Justice, Treasury, Transportation, and Energy; the CIA; and the NSC
Staff, was to be responsive to the SCC. The representative
of the State Department chaired the ECT, and the Deputy
Chairman was a representative from the Department of Justice. The ECT was "especially concerned with the response
to major terrorism incidents and related issues, including periodic testing and evaluation of response capabilities.
The ECT was also responsible for long-range antiterrorism
program planning and analysis."[14]
    In a memo from Zbigniew Brzezinski dated October 20,
1977[15] it was made clear that both the ECT and its Working Group's "primary concern" would be "policy, coordination and information exchange." Neither of the two
was to be charged with the management of specific terrorist incidents. This was to be the function of the lead
agency and, if beyond its scope, the NSC itself.
    The Working Group represented the agencies on the
ECT as well as several others, some with a less direct
involvement in countering terrorism. The WG served "as
a valuable forum for a continuing exchange of practical
information, techniques, and ideas for developing
effective working relationships among key individuals
having responsibility within their agencies for dealing
with terrorism"[16]
    The membership of the Working Group originally (1972)
consisted of 10 agencies:

    Department of State (Chairman)
    Department of the Treasury
    Department of Defense
    Department of Justice
    Department of Transportation
    Central Intelligence Agency
    Federal Bureau of Investigation

National Security Council Staff
U.S. Mission to the U.N.
Domestic Affairs Council Staff[17]

In February 1974, Ambassador Lewis Hoffacker, in his capacity as Special Assistant to the Secretary of State, Coordinator for Combatting Terrorism, was able to advise that ". . . . we are using government-wide resources to better advantage and have at least reduced the risk to our people and our foreign guests."[18]

An indication of the scope of government-wide resources can be garnered from the fact that the Working Group, by early 1975, had added the following agencies to the original 10:[19]

Arms Control & Disarmament Agency
Energy Research & Development Administration
Federal Protective Service (GSA)
Immigration and Naturalization Service
Law Enforcement Assistance Administration
D.C. Metropolitan Police Department
Nuclear Regulatory Commission
National Security Agency
Office of Management and Budget
U.S. Information Agency
Secret Service

By September 1979, Ambassador Quainton could state, "The Working Group represents some 31 Federal Agencies and Departments."[20] (See Figures 4.1 and 4.2).

To obtain a clearer concept of the Working Group and the role of the chairman, the following excerpts from Congressional testimony are presented:

(Conversation between Congressman Don Edwards and Mr. Perry Rivkind, Assistant Administrator, Law Enforcement Assistance Administration, Department of Justice).[21]

Mr. EDWARDS: Mr. Rivkind, the Working Group consists of those agencies that you have described there (ECT)?

Mr. RIVKIND: That, plus approximately 23 more agencies, Mr. Chairman.

Mr. EDWARDS: Are you testifying that there are 40 or 50 members of the working group?

Mr. RIVKIND: There are 27.

Mr. EDWARDS: Do these 27 members meet together?

FIGURE 4.1

Organization for Response to Terrorist Incidents, Carter
Administration

THE PRESIDENT

SPECIAL COORDINATION COMMITTEE (NSC)

National Security Adv   Sec of Defense   Director, CIA
Vice President   Chairman, JCS   Other Concerned
Secretary of State   Agencies

INTERAGENCY POLICY COORDINATION

NSC Staff
Members of Executive Committee with direct interest

INCIDENT MANAGEMENT BY LEAD AGENCY

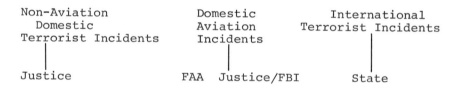

Non-Aviation   Domestic   International
   Domestic   Aviation   Terrorist Incidents
Terrorist Incidents   Incidents

Justice   FAA Justice/FBI   State

Deputy Attorney General   Office for
Emergency Programs Center   Combatting Terrorism

FBI

Source: U.S. Congress, House, Committee on the Judiciary,
Federal Capabilities in Crises Management and Terrorism,
95th Congress, 2nd session, 1978, p. 59.

FIGURE 4.2

Organization for Antiterrorism Planning, Coordination,
and Policy Formulation, Carter Administration

SPECIAL COORDINATION COMMITTEE (NSC)

NSC Adv	Sec of Defense	Director, CIA
Vice President	Chairman, JCS	Other Concerned
Secretary of State		Agencies

EXECUTIVE COMMITTEE ON TERRORISM

State	Treasury	Energy
Justice/FBI	Transportation	NSC Staff
Defense/JCS	CIA	

WORKING GROUP ON TERRORISM

State	Immigration & Naturalization
Justice	Intn'l Communications Agency
ACDA	LEAA
AID	Metropolitan Police Dept
CIA	NSA
Coast Guard	NRC
Commerce	OMB
Customs	Postal Service
Army	Transportation
Defense	FAA
DIA	Treasury
Energy	AT&F (Treasury)
FBI	Secret Service (Treasury)
Fed Preparedness Acy	U.S. Mission to the UN
Fed Protective Svs	HEW
	Joint Chiefs of Staff

COMMITTEES

Research & Development	Public Relations
Security Policy	International Initiatives
Contingency Planning &	
Crisis Management	

Source: U.S. Congress, House, Committee on the Judiciary,
Federal Capabilities in Crises Management and Terrorism,
95th Congress, 2nd session, 1978, p. 60.

Mr. RIVKIND: Yes, they do.

Mr. EDWARDS: How often do they meet?

Mr. RIVKIND: We were meeting, in the past, approximately twice a month.

Mr. EDWARDS: Were 27 people there?

Mr. RIVKIND: More or less, yes. Some brought assistants. There could have been up to 35 on occasion.

Mr. EDWARDS: Is there a chairman or chairperson of the working group?

Mr. RIVKIND: Yes, there is: Ambassador Anthony Quainton.

Mr. EDWARDS: And are minutes kept?

Mr. RIVKIND: They are. The meetings were held twice a month in the past. The Working Group has been reorganized and is now composed of subcommittees which meet separately.

Mr. EDWARDS: What happens at the meetings of the Working Group?

Mr. RIVKIND: In the past general reports on the problems of terrorism were presented. International events that had taken place were reported. There were briefings by various agencies on their role in this area.

Mr. EDWARDS: Thank you.

(Conversation between J.G. Sourwine, Chief Counsel, Subcommittee to Investigate the Administration of the Internal Security Act and other Internal Security Laws, and Ambassador Robert A. Fearey, Coordinator for Combating Terrorism).[22]

Mr. SOURWINE: Would you say that all of the intelligence gathering agencies of the government, including those which only occasionally come into the possession of intelligence, are available to you insofar as they have produced or can produce intelligence that would be useful to your effort?

Mr. FEAREY: Yes. The original directive from President Nixon called for cooperation by all arms of the government in order to further the objectives of the Cabinet Committee.

Mr. SOURWINE: I want to clear up one small point. Who is the present terrorism coordinator of the Department of State?

Mr. FEAREY: I am, sir.

Mr. SOURWINE: So, as you said, you wear two hats and in that capacity do you have, for instance, authority over the Executive Protection Service?

Mr. FEAREY: No, sir. My role is coordinating.

Mr. SOURWINE: You have no rule over the Secret Service?

Mr. FEAREY: No, sir.

Mr. SOURWINE: But there is within your working group as a representative of the Cabinet Committee a person under whom these various smaller organizations come so that your coordination can be pretty effective, can it not?

Mr. FEAREY: Yes. All of these organizations, to the extent their work relates to terrorism, are enjoined by the original letter setting up the structure to work in and through this committee on this topic.

Mr. SOURWINE: I guess what I am trying to get at is whether within the working group you have complete cooperation or whether there is some pulling and hauling between or among agencies.

Mr. FEAREY: No, sir. Of course I am quite new to the activity but my impression is that there has been very good cooperation in the committee.

It was determined that the number of participants in meetings of the Working Group was too large for "the most effective interaction and for drafting or planning." Therefore, "in order to streamline its operations and to maximize its effectiveness in policy coordination," the group was organized based upon functional lines.[23]
The committees were divided as follows:

Research and Development Committee
The committee's overall goals were to coordinate
federal antiterrorism research, respond to research proposals from private individuals and organizations, and
carry out projects assigned by the Working Group and
member agencies.

Security Policy (Domestic) Committee
The committee's work programs included problems
of border management (possible terrorist infiltration
into the United States), interagency exchange of operational information and vulnerability analysis of potential
U.S. targets.

Security Policy (Foreign) Committee
The committee was charged with responsibility for
reviewing past efforts and present plans to strengthen
security at U.S. establishments and residences overseas;
programs to educate and train United States government
employees; programs of assistance to U.S. businessmen
overseas; the effectiveness of the Security Watch Committee concept; and ways in which interagency relationships
might have been made more effective both in Washington
and overseas.

Contingency Planning and Crisis Management (Foreign and Domestic)
The tasks of these committees were to ensure that
agencies had up-to-date contingency plans for incident
management; that command and control relationships among
and between agencies were clearly defined; that crisis managers had the necessary training to carry out their role;
that adequate intelligence was available for crisis management; and that crisis managers had an adequate system of
data storage and retrieval.

Public Information Committee
The committee was to review media guidelines
for coverage of terrorist incidents; consider ways to
prepare government officials to deal with the media during an incident; identify the most useful way to respond
to the present media interest in terrorism; and compile
reference materials dealing with the public information
aspects of terrorism.

International Initiatives Committee
This committee was responsible for exploring all
avenues of multilateral cooperation to control and suppress terrorism; reviewed possible new antiterrorist initiatives at the U.N. or regional organizations; and considered the development of new or modified conventions

relating to hostage-taking, hijacking, or other terrorist
acts.[24]

Due to the number of organizations involved in both
the Working Group and the ECT, an analysis of each and
its role in combating terrorism will not be attempted.
However, since the seven organizations on the ECT were
also in the Working Group, and since each is involved
in the antiterrorist program in the Reagan administration,
their mandates and organizational role will be examined
as they relate to incidents within the U.S.

Department of State

As a result of the NSC's review of the U.S. ability
to counter terror (1977), the State Department's Office
for Combatting Terrorism was given a new mandate to coordinate America's response to both domestic and international
terrorism.[25] Within the executive branch, this office
provides a basic staff for two complementary structures --
one dealing with incident management and the other concerning contingency planning. Additionally, its Communications Operations Center is responsible for the instantaneous communication in the management of crisis
situations. Not only can it reach all parts of the
government, providing direct access to officials, but
it also establishes prompt communications overseas. The
Department of State has a role in collecting and analyzing relevant intelligence data.[26]

Department of Justice

Supervision of the department's response to investigations concerning terrorism was vested in the Deputy
Attorney General, the second-ranking official in the
department. The deputy had supervisory responsibility
over the FBI; the Criminal Division, Law Enforcement
Assistance Administration; and the Immigration and Naturalization Service -- all elements of the department
having a role in the effort to combat terrorism. Under
the Reagan administration these functions are now under
the Associate Attorney General. The FBI is the agency
which exercises principal investigative authority for
criminal violations at the federal level. Public Law
92-539 gives the FBI concurrent jurisdiction with local
agencies in the protection of foreign officials and
official guests. The FBI also has jurisdiction to
investigate nuclear incidents which are of a criminal
or terroristic nature. Nuclear extortions, when there
is threatened use of a device, will be investigated as
extortion and will demand close cooperation between
the FBI, DOD, and DOE. Depending on the circumstances

and timing of the incident, the FBI has primary jurisdiction in hijacking cases. However, when the aircraft
is airborne or in a flying mode, the Federal Aviation
Administration may well have jurisdiction.[27]

Central Intelligence Agency

This organization is the main source of intelligence
on the subject of international terrorism. Little open
data is available concerning the methodology of the
agency in the development of relevant information, especially as it involves the possible use of covert sources
and techniques. Executive Order 12036, issued by President Carter on January 24, 1978, gives the Director of
Central Intelligence authority to develop the National
Foreign Intelligence Program budget and to direct the
tasking of all intelligence community collection elements. In addition to the staff elements of the office
of the Director of Central Intelligence, the community
consists of the CIA, the National Security Agency, the
Defense Intelligence Agency, the military offices concerned with reconnaissance and intelligence programs,
the Bureau of Intelligence and Research of the Department
of State, the FBI, the departments of Treasury and Energy, and the Drug Enforcement Administration.[28]

Department of Defense

The Department of Defense can be viewed as having
two roles to play in countering terrorism. First, it
must protect its own personnel and resources from
attacks. Second, within tightly constrained legal parameters, it can render support to efforts by other federal, state, and local governments. Aside from the constitutional limits on federal government involvement at
the local level, the use of military resources within
the U.S. is prescribed by various statutes. Perhaps the
best known of these is the Posse Comitatus Act which prohibits using Army or Air Force resources to execute or
enforce laws except as authorized by the Constitution
or the Congress. The Department of Defense is authorized
to respond to reasonable FBI requests for material,
facilities, and technical personnel acting to advise and
support FBI responses to terrorist incidents in the United States.[29] The exact role of military force in countering terrorism within a democratic society is a matter
of special interest. It will be explored in some detail
in the following chapter.

Department of Transportation

The primary concern of the department is manifested through the Federal Aviation Administration. The U.S. civil aviation security program currently involves approximately forty U.S. and seventy-five foreign airlines operating in excess of 14,000 scheduled passenger flights each day. With regard to the management of hijacking incidents, the FAA views aviation safety as paramount and seeks to conclude each incident without injury to passengers and crew as well as the prevention of property loss.

The president and the Secretary of Transportation have authority to impose different types of sanctions in the interests of civil air commerce. The president can act against any nation that supports terrorist organizations which use hijacking as an instrument of policy. In addition, the secretary, with the approval of the Secretary of State, can withhold, revoke or impose conditions on the United States operating authorities of the airlines of any nation that does not effectively maintain and administer security measures equal to International Civil Aviation Organization standards.

An ever-increasing appreciation of the role of the U.S. Coast Guard is becoming manifest. To date, most antiterrorist planning has been concerned with land and air domains. With the growth of offshore oil rigs, coupled with their known vulnerability, the need for a quick seaborne response becomes quite evident. In this regard, many jurisdictional issues will have to be worked out with both military and other federal agencies.

Department of the Treasury

The department views its role in countering terrorism not so much from any economic perspective, but, rather because so much law enforcement responsibility comes within its jurisdiction. This would involve three agencies: the U.S. Secret Service, U.S. Customs Service, and Bureau of Alcohol, Tobacco and Firearms (BATF). The Secret Service has protective responsibility for the president, vice president, foreign heads of state when they visit, and major presidential candidates during election periods. Additionally, there is the Uniform Division of the U.S. Secret Service which has responsibility for protecting the White House and foreign embassies in the U.S. The primary goal of these officers would be target protection.

The U.S. Customs Service is mainly concerned with the detection of terrorists attempting to enter the U.S. Further, the identification of the illegal exporting of firearms and munitions also falls under the purview of the Customs Service. However, if false representation or fraud were used to import these weapons, it would also fall within the jurisdiction of BATF. BATF has juris-diction over most bombings; however, when it is reasonably believed that a terrorist is the suspect, then the FBI has prime jurisdiction.

Within the department there is an Assistant Secretary for Enforcement and Operations who has overall policy and program responsibility for all three of the bureaus des-cribed above.[30]

Department of Energy

The department is involved in government nuclear materials management and security. Additionally, the Nuclear Regulatory Commission safeguards activities and has responsibilities which arise from the Atomic Energy Act of 1974 and deals with the commercial sector. While both agencies have a similar mandate, it is important to realize the differences, i.e., government versus commercial. The NRC is an independent regulatory agency under the provisions of the Energy Reorganization Act of 1974 and is not part of DOE. Since this study is con-cerned with those agencies represented on the Executive Committee, it will deal only with DOE.

Within the department is the Nuclear Emergency Search Team (NEST) which, with the assistance of DOD and the FBI, will assist in providing hazard assistance and in neutral-izing nuclear explosive devices.[31] Also in DOE is the Office of Safeguards and Security, under the purview of the Assistant Secretary for Defense Programs, which is responsible for the protection of special nuclear mater-ials and nuclear facilities from theft or sabotage.

Soon after the inauguration of Ronald Reagan a review of the government's counter terrorist effort was undertaken. Secretary of State Alexander Haig initiated this effort to enhance the U.S. ability to meet the per-ceived threat. The result has been the creation of the Interdepartmental Group on Terrorism. Membership remain-ed very similar to the old Executive Committee with the addition of a representative from the office of the vice president. The Department of State continued to be the chair agency. The numerous agencies and departments which comprised the Working Group were discontinued.

With this general appreciation of the governmental organization and structure, we are in a better position to evaluate effectiveness in countering terrorism (Chap-ter 6). Prior to this, however, we will seek to briefly examine the special role played by the Department of De-fense in countering terrorism.

NOTES

1. U.S. Department of State, <u>Bulletin</u>, v. LXVII, no. 1739, October 1972, p. 475.

2. Ibid.

3. Ibid., p. 476.

4. Ibid.

5. Ibid., p. 477. The Committee did not meet again. "In the five years of existence the Committee accomplished little towards fulfilling its mandate." See U.S. Congress, House, <u>Federal Capabilities in Crises Management and Terrorism</u>. Staff Report, Subcommittee on Civil and Constitutional Rights, 95th Congress, 2nd session, December 1978, p. 6.

6. U.S. Congress, Senate, Committee of the Judiciary, <u>Terroristic Activity, International Terrorism Hearings</u> before 1st session, May 14, 1975, p. 215. Testimony by Robert A. Fearey, Special Assistant to the Secretary of State, Coordinator for Combating Terrorism.

7. Ibid., pp. 230-231.

8. Executive Committee on Terrorism, <u>The United States Government Antiterrorist Program</u> (Washington: National Security Council, June 1979), p. 2.

9. Ibid.

10. It must be noted that intelligence gathering concerning terrorist activity is extremely difficult. As was pointed out by then Attorney General Benjamin R. Civiletti, "That is not to suggest at all that we have an ability and capacity, with certainty, to be able to predict terrorist activities. We can't do that well." U.S. Congress, House, Committee on the Judiciary. <u>Federal Capabilities in Crises Management and Terrorism Hearings</u> before a subcommittee of the Committee on the Judiciary, House of Representatives, 95th Congress, 2nd session, 1978, p. 14.

11. Executive Committee on Terrorism, p. 7.

12. For a view of the way the NSC used to function, see John Leacocus, "Kissinger's Apparat," <u>Foreign Policy</u>, No. 5, 1971, pp. 2-24.

13. U.S. Congress, House, Committee on International Relations, Subcommittee on International Security and Scientific Affairs, <u>International Terrorism: Legislative Initiatives</u>, Hearing on H. R. 13387, September 12, 1978, pp. 2-3.

14. Executive Committee on Terrorism, p. 7.

15. Memo from Zbigniew Brzezinski dated October 20, 1977, supplementing his September 16, 1977 memo, establishing the NSC/SCC Working Group on Terrorism.

16. Testimony by Ambassador Quainton, before a subcommittee of the Committee of the Judiciary, 1978, p. 36.

17. Testimony By Ambassador Fearey, p. 215.

18. Hearings before a subcommittee of the Committee of the Judiciary, May 15, 1975, p. 248.

19. Testimony by Ambassador Fearey, p. 215.

20. U.S. Department of State, Bulletin, v. 79, no. 2030, September 1979, p. 63.

21. Testimony by Perry Rivkind before a subcommittee of the Committee of the Judiciary, 1978, pp. 64-65.

22. Testimony by Ambassador Fearey, p. 228.

23. Testimony by Ambassador Quainton before a subcommittee of the Committee of the Judiciary, 1978, p. 36.

24. Letter from Douglas J. Bennet, Jr., Assistant Secretary for Congressional Relations, to Don Edwards, House of Representatives, December 14, 1978.

25. Bulletin, September 1979, p. 62.

26. U.S. Congress, Senate, Committee on Governmental Affairs, An Act to Combat Terrorism, report to accompany S. 2236, 1978, pp. 28-29.

27. Ibid., pp. 32-33.

28. U.S. Central Intelligence Agency, Central Intelligence Agency Fact Book (Washington: undated), p. 9.

29. U.S. Congress, Senate, Committee on Governmental Affairs, An Act to Combat Terrorism, report to accompany S. 2236, 1978, pp. 29-31

30. Interview with Robert McBrien, Office of the Assistant Secretary for Enforcement and Operations, U.S. Department of the Treasury, Washington: February 13, 1980.

31. Center for Policy Research, National Governors' Association, Domestic Terrorism (Washington: U.S. Govt. Print. Off., May 1979), p. 104.

5
Aspects of
Military Involvement

The possible employment of American military forces
in a large-scale domestic terrorist incident is a matter
worthy of consideration. Such use of forces would entail
significant legal decisions made in light of the role
played by the military in American society. Before ex-
pounding on the actual capabilities of existing forces,
it is necessary to examine other factors in some detail.

In the comparatively recent period since the beginning of World War II, the American military establishment has passed through several distinctive phases.[1]
Before the war, the military forces constituted less
than one percent of the male labor force and were strictly
volunteers. The enlisted force was composed mainly of
people from working-class or rural origins, while officers
were drawn predominately from southern, Protestant, middle-
class families. Socially, the pre-World War II military
was self-contained and markedly separated from civilian
society.

By 1945 close to twelve million people were in uniform,
a large majority of whom were assigned to combat and service units. While these forces were socially representative of American society, the military remained an institution whose organization contrasted starkly with existing civilian structures. A large demobilization took place
after the conflict, only to reverse itself to a ceiling
of 3.6 million men at the height of the Korean War. Organizationally and materially, the armed forces of this war
closely resembled those of World War II.

The military of the Cold War, which averaged 2.5
million, was composed increasingly of those with some form
of technical specialization. The proportion of people
assigned to combat or service units declined markedly with
the corresponding increase of electronic and technical
specialists. The war in Vietnam illustrated yet another
phase of the armed forces in American society. Not only
was the war itself opposed by many, but the basic legiti-
macy of military service was brought into question.
Coupled with the antiwar feeling were the revelations of

atrocities and ecological devastation in Vietnam. Adding to these woes were the reports of widespread drug abuse, corruption in the operation of clubs, cost overruns, and military spying on civilian political activists.

> The contrast in ideological and public evaluation of the American military establishment over three wars is revealing. In World War II, the American military was almost universally held in high esteem in a popularly supported war. Conservative and isolationist sectors of American public opinion were quick to fall in line behind a liberal and interventionist national leadership. In the wake of the Korean war, defamatory images of the American serviceman were propagated by right-wing spokesmen. Liberal commentators, on the other hand, generally defended the qualities of the American armed forces. In the war in Southeast Asia a still different image emerged. Although initially an outcome of a liberal Administration, the war came to be primarily defended by political conservatives, while the severest attacks on both the behavior of American soldiers and the military establishment emanated from the left.[2]

As the above discussion would indicate, the employment of military force within the domestic arena could well depend upon society's view of the military as an acceptable institution. A president would be loathe to call in the military to quell a domestic incident when the presence of men and women in uniform could greatly exacerbate the existing turmoil.

Coupled with the concern for the perceptual considerations of the military as an institution is yet another serious aspect. Having once accepted the military as a valid (needed) part of society, the role it would be allowed to play in maintaining domestic security had to be examined. Many of the founding fathers considered that the arbitrary use of military force by the British was a factor contributing to the Revolution. By the separation of powers and the use of constitutional checks and balances, the control of the military was divided between the federal government and the states on the one hand and between branches within the government on the other.[3] While many people have viewed these constitutional efforts as attempts to prevent the military from gaining too much political control, at least one author takes a different and very interesting view:

> The Framers' concept of civilian control was to control the uses to which civilians might

put military force rather than to control the
military themselves. They were more afraid
of military power in the hands of political
officials than of political power in the
hands of military officers.[4]

If there was a struggle for control of the military,
it was not between the armed forces and civilians. Rather,
it was a struggle between the Congress and the president.
The chief executive identified civilian control with
presidential control, while Congress viewed it as congressional control.[5]
Whatever one's perspective, this congressional/exec-
utive power struggle has made political involvement with
the military a matter of routine. While the executive
branch has been generally in control since the end of
World War II, Congress more recently has made vigorous
efforts to regain some of that power (e.g., the 1973 War
Powers Resolution) and reassert greater congressional
control over the military. Such activity additionally
provides the military an opportunity to take advantage
of any political involvement.

As both parties to this struggle have maneuv-
ered for an advantage, the military itself
has been drawn into the controversy. Each
side seeks to enlist the support and assistance of military leaders, the services, and
even the entire profession. Executive Branch
leaders call upon the Joint Chiefs of Staff
and senior commanders to support Administration proposals for reorganizing the Defense
Department, while congressional committees
call upon the service chiefs and their dep-
uties to oppose Defense Department efforts
to increase centralized control over the
services by the Office of the Secretary of
Defense. As a result, the military is com-
pelled to become involved in what is essentially a political power struggle -- a power
struggle that takes the form of disputes
over policy decisions. In (Samuel) Huntington's words, 'The separation of powers'
between Congress and the President 'is a
perpetual invitation, if not an irresis-
tible force, drawing military leaders into
political conflicts.'

What we have, then, is a military that has been
involved consistently in politics. The armed forces
have not been an isolated segment of the population but
rather, an element very much subject to and a participant

in our political system. Its role within our society
has been the subject of much interpretation, both
favorable and unfavorable. It is within these political
and societal parameters that the president must make his
choice for eventual employment in a domestic terrorist
incident.

Legal Rationale

The current state of constitutional and statutory
law severely limits the use of military forces in
domestic situations. The authority to order the intervention of federal troops in domestic law enforcement
generally centers on the office of the president.
The strongest legal prohibition against the use of
military force to execute civil and criminal law is
Title 18, Section 1385, of the U.S. Code, Use of Army
and Air Force as Posse Comitatus (power of the country).
This provides that whoever, except under circumstances
expressly authorized by the Constitution or Congress,
willfully uses any part of the above-stated forces as a
posse comitatus or otherwise to execute the laws shall be
fined not more than $10,000 or imprisoned not more than
two years or both. The Act was originally passed in
1878 as the result of the use of U.S. troops by President
Grant "to secure the better execution of the laws" during
the election of 1876.[7] During debates in Congress at
the time it was argued that the Army had been used improp-
erly to execute local laws, control strikes and collect
taxes. It was argued that these improper actions had
been performed at the behest of U.S. attorneys and law
enforcement agents.

> Various Army reports were cited showing that
> in 1871 four companies helped collect revenue
> in New York, that from 1871 through 1875 there
> were more than 441 reported incidents in Ken-
> tucky in which soldiers were called out to aid
> federal and state law enforcement authorities,
> and that in 1876 at least 71 detachments of
> soldiers aided civil authorities.[8]

Originally the Posse Comitatus legislation prohibited only the Army from aiding civil authorities. In
1956 the Act was added to Title 18 of the U.S. Code,
and the Air Force was included to reflect earlier legislation separating the two services. There has been a
good deal of controversy resulting from the fact that
the Navy (to include Marines) has not been specifically
included. While there was extensive debate for years on
this issue, the Secretary of the Navy clarified the matter in 1974 when he issued a directive forbidding Navy

and Marine Corps personnel from enforcing or executing
local, state, or federal civil law in violation of the
Posse Comitatus Act.[9]

The U.S. Coast Guard is under the jurisdiction of
the Navy during war and therefore would be controlled by
the Act. However, during times of peace it is not completely clear exactly how the Act would apply inasmuch as
the Coast Guard is under the jurisdiction of the Department of Transportation.[10]

As indicated earlier, the president could call into
federal service the militia of any state and such armed
forces as he considers necessary to suppress "unlawful
obstructions, combinations or assemblages, or rebellion"
against the authority of the United States or any state
in particular.[11]

This authority is contained in the Constitution
which states:

> . . . . He shall receive ambassadors and other
> public ministers; he shall take care that the
> laws be faithfully executed, and shall commis-
> sion all the officers of the United States.[12]

> The United States shall guarantee to every
> state in this Union a republican form of gov-
> ernment and shall protect each of them against
> invasion; and on application of the legisla-
> ture, or of the executive (when the legislature
> cannot be convened) against domestic violence.[13]

> No State shall make or enforce any law which
> shall abridge the privileges or immunities
> of citizens of the United States; nor shall
> any State deprive any person of life, liber-
> ty, or property without due process of law;
> nor deny to any person within its jurisdic-
> tion the equal protection of the laws.[14]

The following federal statutes allow the president
to use federal troops under certain conditions:

> Whenever there is an insurrection in any State
> against its government, the President may,
> upon request of its legislature or of its
> governor if the legislature cannot be convened,
> call into federal service such of the militia
> of the other States, in the number requested
> by that State, and use such of the Armed For-
> ces, as he considers necessary to suppress
> the insurrection.[15]

Whenever the President considers that unlawful obstructions, combinations, or assemblages, or rebellion against the authority of the United States, make it impracticable to enforce the laws of the United States in any State or Territory by the ordinary course of judicial proceedings, he may call into federal service such of the militia of any State, and use such of the Armed Forces, as he considers necessary to enforce those laws or to suppress the rebellion.[16]

The President, by using the militia or the Armed Forces, or both, or by any other means, shall take such measures as he considers necessary to suppress, in a State, any insurrection, domestic violence, unlawful combination, or conspiracy, if it -

(1) so hinders the execution of the laws of that State, and of the United States within the State, that any part or class of its people is deprived of a right, privilege, immunity, or protection named in the Constitution and secured by law, and the constituted authorities of that State are unable, fail, or refuse to protect that right, privilege, or immunity, or to give that protection; or

(2) opposes or obstructs the execution of the laws of the United States or impedes the course of justice under those laws.

In any situation covered by clause (1), the State shall be considered to have denied the equal protection of the laws secured by the Constitution.[17]

Although the Posse Comitatus Act prevents the use of federal troops to enforce federal or state laws without constitutional or statutory authorization, it does not forbid the loan of military material and equipment to federal law enforcement agencies in connection with a continuing civil disorder.

In United States vs. Red Feather (one of the Wounded Knee cases)[18] the court ruled that the loan of military equipment was not a violation of the Act. The court went one step further, outlining the differences between the use of federal troops in an active role of executing the laws and the passive role in which they would indirectly aid civilian law enforcement by saying:

Based on the clear intent of Congress, this
court holds that the clause 'to execute the
laws,' contained in 18 U.S.C.: 1385 makes unlawful the use of federal military troops in
an active role of direct law enforcement by
civil law enforcement officers. Activities
which constitute an active role in direct law
enforcement are: arrest; seizure of evidence;
search of a person; search of crime; inter-
viewing witnesses; pursuit of an escaped civilian prisoner; search of an area for a suspect and other like activities. . . .

However,

Activities which constitute a passive role
which might indirectly aid law enforcement
are: mere presence of military personnel
under orders to report on the necessity for
military intervention; preparation of contingency plans to be used if military intervention is ordered; advice or recommendations
given to civilian law enforcement officers
by military personnel on tactics or logis-
tics; presence of military personnel to
deliver military material, equipment or
supplies, to train local law enforcement
officials on the proper use and care of such
material or equipment, and to maintain such
material or equipment; aerial photographic
reconnaissance flights and other like activities.[19]

Legal Difficulties

While certain aspects of the law are clear, there
are others that are undergoing close examination to remove
ambiguities. Both the Department of Justice and the
Department of Defense continue attempts to come to grips
with this uncertainty in efforts to coordinate their
preparations for and response to domestic terrorism.[20]
The actions considered center on the use of military
force with their civilian counterparts before actual
use of the armed forces has been authorized under the
provisions outlined above, since, prior to their being
invoked, the Posse Comitatus Act forbids civilian authorities from using the military to carry out their own responsibilities.
One aspect of concern for the military is to determine at what point military observers could be sent to
the location of an event without violating the law. The
Department of Justice appears to endorse the finding of

the United States vs. Red Feather case while indicating
that some disagreement exists as to what additional activities the military observer could engage in (e.g., maintenance of equipment as it is being used by civilian
authorities) without going beyond the limits of the law.
Mere presence at the scene would not be viewed as a violation of the Posse Comitatus Act. It was also noted that
in the court's review of the cases resulting from the
Wounded Knee incident,[21] it was not explicitly set forth
that the impending use of military force was needed as a
justification for the presence of military observers. Concern had also been voiced about the propriety of liaison
for the purpose of sharing intelligence concerning a terrorist incident. The prevailing thought is that the prohibition of use of the military by civilian authorities to
execute laws does not bar contact for the sole purpose of
enabling the military to obtain knowledge relating to a
situation. If it appears that it may be necessary to
preposition troops in anticipation of their actual employment, such prepositioning is not determined to involve
actual enforcement and, therefore, would not be considered
illegal. Likewise, reconnaissance by the military, independent of civilian law enforcement, would be considered
legal in the sense that it was done with the expectation
that forces would be needed to augment local authorities.

The foregoing discussion indicates that the use of
military force must be an option taken after due consideration of the social, legal and political context of an
incident. The president, satisfied that the employment
of military force is needed, would issue the necessary
orders through the Secretary of the Army who is the executive agent for the use of military forces in civil
disturbances. These forces are assigned or committed to
him through the Chief of Staff, U.S. Army (CSA).[22]

The concept of operations involved is detailed in
the Department of the Army Civil Disturbance Plan, Garden Plot, which provides for the employment of military
forces in times of civil disturbances within the fifty
states, the District of Columbia, the Commonwealth of
Puerto Rico, and U.S. territories or possessions.[23] The
definition of a terrorist incident as defined in the
plan is extremely broad, providing considerable latitude
for interpretation.[24] Military commanders who have been
delegated the authority to supply equipment, in those
cases where it may be difficult to determine whether an
incident falls into the terrorist category, are "authorized
to accept the judgement of the FBI official making the
request if it is supported by available facts." The FBI
official does not have to be the director but may well
be the senior agent on the scene.[25]

As a matter of policy, the FBI has been given overall
jurisdictional responsibility at the locus of a terrorist

incident wherever it occurs, including military installations.

Department of Defense components are authorized to
respond to reasonable requests of the FBI for military
resources. The form of assistance may include material,
facilities, and technical personnel acting in an advisory
capacity. As noted above, military personnel could not
be used in a law enforcement role outside a military in-
stallation without presidential authorization. While
troops can be made available to the FBI with approval of
the president, command and operational control would remain with the military.

Requests for training, long-term loans of equipment,
and other requests not based on imminent threats or ongoing incidents would be forwarded through FBI and Department of Justice (DOJ) channels for submission by DOJ to
the Secretary of the Army.

Procedurally, the secretaries of the military departments, commanders of military installations or organizations with delegated authority, and the commanders-in-
chief of unified and specified commands outside CONUS
could grant requests for riot control agents, concertina
wire, fire fighting resources, protective equipment,
clothing, communications gear, searchlights, explosive
ordnance disposal, and detector dog teams. Other items
not prohibited could be provided.

Although circumstances will determine the order in
which various forces are employed, it is envisioned that
first local and state police would be used, followed by
Army and Air National Guard under state control and, finally, federal military forces.[26]

The commitment of federal military forces as set
forth in Garden Plot has been viewed as a drastic last
resort and their role should never be greater than abso-
lutely necessary under the particular circumstances that
prevail. Firepower is to be limited, with only semiauto-
matic weapons used. Where automatic weapons must be employed, they will not be fired automatically, except on
order of competent authority as delegated by the task
force commander.[27]

Since the use of deadly force invokes the power of
summary execution it can be justified only in extreme
necessity. Its use is not authorized for the purpose of
preventing activities that do not pose a significant risk
of death or serious bodily harm.[28]

Having set forth the prohibition on the use of force
under Posse Comitatus, two significant exceptions must
also be addressed. Under certain circumstances, readily
conceiveable, military force can be employed domestically
without presidential proclamation.

As a result of the Organization of American States "Convention to Prevent and Punish the Acts of Terrorism Taking the Form of Crimes Against Persons and Related Extortion that are of International Significance" and the UN "Convention on the Prevention of Crimes Against Internationally Protected Persons," the U.S. Congress had to pass legislation to insure their implementation. It is standing policy of the State Department not to deposit an instrument of ratification unless it is assured that federal law would permit the United States to fully discharge its treaty obligations. The safeguards of this legislation not only pertain to heads of state but also to:

> Any representative or official of a State or any official or other agent of an international organization of an intergovernmental character who, at the time when and in the place where a crime against him, his official premises, his private accommodations or his means of transport, is committed, is entitled pursuant to international law to special protection from any attack on his person, freedom or dignity, as well as members of his family forming part of his household.[29]

Additionally, the legislation authorized "The Attorney General, in the course of enforcing the provisions of the statute relating to internationally protected persons, to request assistance from any federal, state, or local agency."[30] Specifically, the law reads:

> In the course of enforcement of this and any other sections prohibiting a conspiracy or attempt to violate this section, the Attorney General may request assistance from any Federal, State, or local agency, including the Army, Navy and the Air Force, any statute, rule, or regulation to the contrary notwithstanding.[31]

This particular piece of legislation's provisions parallel part of Public Law 91-644 passed in 1971 dealing with congressional assassination, kidnapping, and assault. That law stated that whoever kills or kidnaps (or attempts same) any individual who is a member of Congress or a member of Congress-elect shall be punished and

> Violations of this section shall be investigated by the Federal Bureau of Investigation. Assistance may be requested from any Federal, State, or local agency, including the Army, Navy, and

Air Force, any statute, rule, or regulation to
the contrary notwithstanding.[32]

In their concern to protect foreign dignitaries and
themselves, members of Congress enacted two laws which
provide a basis for overriding the letter and intent of
Posse Comitatus. It is interesting to note that the implications of this fact were not completely realized by
members of the Executive Committee on Terrorism until
1980, when a legal advisor in the Department of State
brought it to their attention. As one participant at
the meeting described the impact on most present, "It was
profound."[33]
          While it is not expected that the military would, in
fact, be called up without the president being informed,
it is a vastly different situation than the need for presidential authority for such action. It is interesting to
speculate as to the stand of the Department of Defense in
such a situation. Two strong tides would be drawing on
the decision makers: the continuance of the long standing tradition of abstaining from civil affairs versus the
opportunity to successfully (it is hoped) prove, in the
wake of the Iranian mission, that a true counterterror
capability exists within the armed forces.

Military Capabilities

          Garden Plot provides the basis for planning
the use of military personnel and equipment to respond
to terrorist acts. What the plan does not indicate is the
full complement of military capability. This issue of
capability, not only as it pertains to the military but
also to the entire federal spectrum, has been the subject
of intense discussion. Specialists in the field and
high-ranking officers familiar with the activities have
repeatedly contended that the United States antiterrorist
competence is relatively weak.[34]
          In response to questions raised by the Committee on
Government Affairs of the United States Senate, Assistant
Secretary of Defense for International Security Affairs,
David E. McGiffert, gave testimony relative to United
States capability for dealing with terrorists. At these
hearings on the Omnibus Antiterrorism Act, Senator John
Glenn asked about United States capabilities similar to
those displayed by Israel's Saiyeret at Entebbe, the
West German Grenzschutzgruppe-9 at Mogadishu and the
Egyptian commando force at Cyprus. The reply was that,
although never activated as of that time to counter a
terrorist threat or act, U.S. forces consisted of Army,
Navy and Air Force units trained in counterterrorism.
Further, the emphasis on training was for employment
abroad because use of Army personnel domestically "would

require waiver by the president of the <u>Posse Comitatus</u> Act."[35] These forces were described as "specially trained military" which are among the resources of the Department of Defense available as "may be appropriate in a terrorist situation."[36]

Such testimony could have been interpreted as the United States having available a strike force that is comparable to the West German Border Protection Group Nine (G.S.G. - 9), which was formed as a result of the Munich Olympic massacre. Under the leadership of Ulrich Wegener, the G.S.G. - 9 might be one of the most formidable antiterrorist groups in the world. Each member of the group must be a volunteer, capable of maintaining calmness under the most severe stress, and possess a minimum I.Q. of 110. Rigorous training in martial arts, hand combat, scuba diving and special weapons use has built a team capable of quick, decisive action as exemplified by the success at Mogadishu.

Other countries have also formed specialist antiterrorist teams, such as the British Special Air Service (SAS) that was created during World War II and used successfully in London in 1980. The French have a highly respected thirty-man team, the <u>Gigene</u>, and the Italians formed a fifty-man <u>Squadra Anti-Commando</u>.[37]

Compared to these "lean and mean" units, the United States identified the following U.S. military forces as having counterterrorist capabilities:[38]

1. U.S. Army Ranger Battalions

    -- 588 men
    -- Located at Fort Stewart, GA, and Fort
       Lewis, WA.

2. USMC Battalion Landing Team

    -- 1200 men
    -- Located at Camp LeJeune, NC, Camp
       Pendleton, CA, and on Okinawa
    -- Can be air-landed

3. USMC Marine Amphibious Unit

    -- 1800 men
    -- Located in WESTPAC* and Mediterranean
       (afloat)
    -- Immediately available but location varies
    -- Can be landed by helicopters

*West Pacific

4. U.S. Army Special Forces

-- Nine battalions of 242 men
-- Located at Fort Bragg, NC (5), Fort
   Devens, MA (2), Canal Zone (1), and
   FRG (1)
-- Response time varies depending on
   current operations/training missions
   underway
-- Parachute qualified
-- Language qualified for many areas

5. U.S. Marine Force Reconnaissance Company

-- One company of 190 men
-- Located at Camp LeJeune, NC
-- Parachute, scuba qualified
-- Extensive training suitable for
   counterterrorist operations

6. U.S. Navy, Sea, Air, Land (SEAL) Platoons

-- Nineteen platoons of 14 men each
-- Located at Little Creek, VA (7),
   Coronada, CA (10), and Subic Bay, PH (2)
-- Capable of infiltration/exfiltration
   by submarine, boat, ship, aircraft,
   and parachute

7. Air Force Support

-- Special mission aircraft
-- Combat Talon -- nap-of-the-earth
   penetration methods. Located in
   Florida, Okinawa, and Germany
-- Combat spectre gunships located in
   Florida

It is obvious from this listing that the U.S. forces
that have been designated are heavy in terms of men, equipment, and firepower when compared to their European counterparts.

McGiffert's testimony to the Senate subcommittee
further stated that:

-- Depending on the nature of the mission
   the size of U.S. military forces may
   range from a small element to a larger
   task force

-- Force size is scenario-dependent and the
   division of labor between units is tail-

ored to specific circumstances and technical requirements

-- Counterterrorist exercises have been conducted.[39]

In terms of planning:

-- The JCS has developed plans to provide
for U.S. military operations to counter
terrorist activities overseas.

-- There are a number of terrorist acts that
might trigger a U.S. military response.
Possible military missions range from the
rescue of hostages from a hijacked U.S.
aircraft to recovery/neutralization/des-
truction of stolen nuclear weapons.[40]

Yet one analysis of the degree of U.S. preparations led
its authors to contend that:

Today, the United States has no single unit
equivalent to the West German Border Group
Nine (Grenzschutzgruppe Neun or G.S.G. - 9
for short), successful at Mogadishu, which is
authorized to act outside of our borders in
response to terrorist action aimed at American
interests or citizens abroad. Domestically,
we have three degrees of antiterrorist capabilities: First, some local police departments
have developed and fielded antiterrorist units.
At the second level of slightly higher response,
we find a few state and Federal special teams
and armed forces elements with limited special
training. Whether the state units could operate internationally or the military could perform domestically is questionable, but at least
the raw resource is recognized and present to
some degree. At the highest tier, that of transnational terrorism, however, there is a cloud.[41]

Both the authors of this study and others have made
reference to "Blue Light." The term possibly came from
the flash of the stun grenades that were used at Mogadishu. Other authors assigned the name Operation Blue
Light to a combined force of Army, Navy, Air Force, and
Marine personnel. It has been written that the force
called Blue Light was one established by order of President Carter in March 1978. The force, under command of
Col. Charles Beckwith, was 200 personnel strong, given special weapons and training, and was to be retained as a spec-

ialized force.[42] Newsweek magazine also reported in 1977
that the Pentagon maintained two special 600-man Black
Beret Army Ranger battalions at Fort Stewart, Georgia,
and Fort Lewis, Washington.[43]

The true nature of the U.S. military counterterrorism
capability began to unfold in 1980 in the wake of the
aborted Iranian rescue mission. The impression created
by the testimony of McGiffert was shattered like the
wreckage of the aircraft left behind in the desert. The
review report presented by Admiral (Ret.) James L. Holloway, III, provided a narrative of the events leading
up to the mission and a clear indictment of many aspects
of the operation.[44]

Immediately following the hostage seizure, a small
planning cell working at the Pentagon and augmented by
two officers from the ground rescue force (described
above under the command of Col. Beckwith) began to formulate concepts for military operations as directed by the
Chairman, Joint Chiefs of Staff (JCS). During the early
stages, existing JCS contingency plans were employed only
relating to the utilization of intelligence assets and
the selection of the ground rescue force. Other significant areas, such as organization planning, integration of
concurrent planning by subordinate units and the determination of support requirements were compartmentalized
and based upon ad hoc arrangements.

Training was quickly undertaken and the helicopter
option was recommended as having the best chances of success. An Air Force general was appointed as a special
advisor to the task force based upon his recent experience
in Iran. The senior Marine officer involved in the operation was assigned to the Office of the Chairman, JCS,
and while not officially designated a member of the rescue
task force, became actively involved in mission planning
especially relating to helicopter training.

It was implied that this officer was in charge
of the helicopter force during the preparation
phase, and he believed this to be so. However,
COMJTF (Commander Joint Task Force) may have
thought differently, and it was evident the
first two months of training that much (if not
all) of the COMJTF effort concerning helicopter
preparation and special mission capability was
done through the general officer who was thought
to be the consultant on Iran. In mid-January
1980, the role of the senior Marine had evolved
into that of overall helicopter force leader,
and since no other designation had been made,
and at his request, he began to attend the
COMJTF planning meetings.[45]

The officer who served as the Deputy Commander of
the Air Force component was just prior to (mission)
execution designated on scene commander at the desert
site:

> implying a command, control and commun-
> cations (C^3) capability to exercise command.
> This was not fully provided. A general officer
> served primarily as a consultant on Iran from
> late November 1979 to mid-February 1980. He
> spent considerable time during this period at
> the western training site in the western United
> States monitoring helicopter and other air
> training. On 12 April 1980, he was delegated
> the Deputy COMJTF.[46]

Additionally, the Holloway group faulted the operations
security as being too stringent, causing excessive com-
partmentalization and planning review by those who had
actually drawn up the original plans.[47] The available
existing intelligence assets were seen as being de-
ficiently managed and integrated.[48] Training activity
was faulted as being too decentralized,[49] and lacking
overall management.[50] Communications between the
helicopters and transport aircraft at the desert rendez-
vous were all seen as deficient in some respects.[51]
Finally, the size of the helicopter force and the accuracy
of weather data were criticized by the review group.[52]
On the positive side the report noted:

> We are, nevertheless, apprehensive that the
> critical tone of our discussion could be mis-
> interpreted as an indictment of the able and
> brave men who planned and executed this op-
> eration. We encountered not a shred of evi-
> dence of culpable neglect or incompetence.
> The facts are that, in the conduct of
> this review, we have seen infinitely more to
> be proud of than to complain about. The
> American servicemen who participated in
> this mission -- the planner, crewman, or
> trooper -- deserved to have a successful
> outcome. It was the ability, dedication,
> and enthusiasm of these people who made what
> everyone thought was an impossibility into
> what should have been a success.
> Finally, we were often reminded that only
> the United States military, alone in the world,
> had the ability to accomplish what the United
> States planned to do. It was risky and we
> knew it, but it had a good chance of success
> and America had the courage to try.[53]

In the late summer of 1980 the Department of Defense announced that it would establish a counterterrorist task force with specialists from the Army, Navy, Air Force, and Marines. The unit is to be responsible for gathering information concerning the tactics and operations from other special groups such as the British SAS and the West German G.S.G.-9. Should an incident take place the unit would allegedly put together a strike force from the military services according to the needs of a specific mission.[54] The core of this counterterror capability is said to be the few hundred commandos of the Army's Delta Team headquartered at Fort Bragg, North Carolina.[55]

The Joint Chiefs of Staff also has organized a panel of senior officers, both active and retired, to oversee training and operational plans.[56] Further information concerning the size, scope, and capabilities cannot be addressed since the entire effort is classified.

The United States in the early 1980s finds itself on the horns of a dilemma. President Reagan has pledged swift and effective retribution against acts of international terrorism directed against the United States. However, the ability of this nation to conduct a military response has been attempted only once and the effort was unsuccessful. Though some have argued that the failure centered on a logistical problem not likely to occur again, the result remains the same. Secretary of Defense Caspar W. Weinberger ennunciated his difficulty in testimony before Congress when he advised that "describing the country's antiterrorist capabilities might compromise a future operation, but that keeping them secret was preventing him from sending a strong message to potential terrorists."[57]

In the previous chapter it was pointed out that deterrence is one of the four main blocks of the U.S. strategy to counter terrorism. Integral to deterrence strategy are capability, credibility, and communication. This requires that those seeking to employ this concept need to communicate their capability to insure its credibility to the adversary.[58] Thus, the decision faced by Secretary Weinberger was indeed a difficult one.

Having presented the governmental structure to combat terrorism as well as the unique role of the military in that effort, we will now turn to the scope of terrorist activity as it affects this country to demonstrate the need for a U.S. response.

NOTES

1. Charles C. Moskos, Jr., "The Emergent Military: Civil, Traditional, or Pluralistic?" in John E. Endicott and Roy W. Stafford, Jr., eds., American Defense Policy

(Baltimore: Johns Hopkins University Press, 1977) pp. 527-537.

2. Ibid., pp. 528-529.

3. John H. Garrison, "The Political Dimension of Military Professionalism," in John E. Endicott and Roy W. Stafford, Jr., eds., American Defense Policy (Baltimore: Johns Hopkins University Press, 1977), p. 582.

4. Ibid.

5. Ibid.

6. Ibid., p. 583.

7. Clarence I. Meeks, "Illegal Law Enforcement: Aiding Civil Authorities in Violation of the Posse Comitatus Act," Military Law Review, v. 70, Fall 1975, pp. 83, 91-92.

8. Ibid., p. 92. It should be noted that the vote to pass the act was fairly close: 130 to 117 with 44 abstentions.

9. Ibid., p. 103.

10. Robert L. Rabe, "Crisis Management of Terrorist Incidents: Legal Aspects and Issues," Unpublished paper, copyright 1979 by author, p. 14.

11. Ibid.

12. U.S. Constitution, Article 2, Section 3.

13. U.S. Constitution, Article 4, Section 4.

14. U.S. Constitution, Article 14, Section 1.

15. 10 U.S. Code 331 (1973).

16. 10 U.S. Code 332 (1973).

17. 10 U.S. Code 333 (1973).

18. These cases stemmed from the takeover of the hamlet of Wounded Knee on the Oglala Sioux reservation in South Dakota by armed supporters of the American Indian Movement (AIM), February 1973. They sought a review of the 371 treaties between the U.S. government and the Sioux Indians. Additionally, there was also concern for alleged corruption within the Bureau of Indian Affairs. The seventy-day confrontation ended in May of that year with the government promising an intensive investigation into the complaints. Several people were killed and wounded during the incident.

19. Rabe, p. 17.

20. The content of this and the next several paragraphs is based upon interviews of personnel assigned to the Department of Defense's Office of International Security Affairs and the Department of Justice's Emergency Programs Center.

21. Meeks, pp. 83-136. During the civil disturbances at Wounded Knee, South Dakota (March 1973), the Department of Defense sent an Army colonel to observe the disorders instigated by the members of the American Indian Movement. As an observer he was not violating the Posse Comitatus Act; however, the officer actually

became an advisor to the civil law enforcement agents, giving advice on rules of engagement, negotiation and placement of equipment. He also obtained another active duty Army colonel to assist with logistical support. The judge in the Red Feather case concluded that the colonels' advice (as well as the aid given by the vehicle mechanics and pilots) was passive involvement. He reasoned that only active involvement such as participation in arrest, search of persons and places, seizure of evidence and the pursuit of escaped prisoners violates the Act. However, both the DOJ and DOD in policy statements tend to back away from the Red Feather case and state that the use of equipment loaned to civil authorities would be authorized but that operators "employed in connection with loaned equipment may not be used in a direct law enforcement role." This matter is still not clearly resolved and may yet require further judicial review.

22. U.S. Department of the Army, DA Civil Disturbance Plan (Garden Plot), August 3, 1978, Headquarters, Washington, DC, p. 1.

23. Ibid., p. C-2.

24. Ibid., p. 0-1. A terrorist incident "is defined as a distinct criminal act committed or threatened to be committed by a group or single individual in order to advance a political objective, and greatly endangering safety or property."

25. Ibid., p. 0-2.

26. Ibid., p. C-1.

27. Ibid., p. C-10-1.

28. Ibid.

29. United States Code, Congressional and Administrative News, 94th Congress, Second Session, Volume 4 (St. Paul, West Publishing Co., 1976), p. 4481.

30. Ibid., p. 4483.

31. United States Code, Congressional and Administrative News, 94th Congress, Second Session, Volume 2, Public Laws 94-456 to 94-588 (St. Paul, West Publishing Co., 1976), p. 1998.

32. United States Code, Annotated, Title 18, Crimes and Criminal Procedure, Unannotated Text (St. Paul, West Publishing Co., 1970), p. 16.

33. Interview with a member of the Executive Committee on Terrorism, November 14, 1980.

34. The New York Times, April 23, 1978, p. 14.

35. David E. McGiffert, "Testimony," U.S. Congress, Senate, Committee on Governmental Affairs, An Act to Combat International Terrorism, Hearings (Washington: U.S. Govt. Print. Off., 1978), p. 192.

36. Ibid., pp. 191-192.

37. Newsweek, October 31, 1977, p. 51.

38. McGiffert, p. 195.

68

39. Ibid., p. 197.

40. Ibid.

41. C. S. Del Grosso and John C. Short, "A Concept for Antiterrorist Operations," Marine Corps Gazette, June 1979, p. 54.

42. Christopher Dobson and Ronald Payne, The Terrorists (New York: Facts on File, 1979), pp. 144-145.

43. Newsweek, October 31, 1977, p. 51.

44. James L. Holloway, III, et al., "Rescue Mission Report," Unpublished paper dated August 1980, pp. 15-16.

45. Ibid., p. 16.

46. Ibid., pp. 16-17.

47. Ibid., p. 13.

48. Ibid., p. 20.

49. Ibid., p. 23.

50. Ibid., p. 25.

51. Ibid., p. 29.

52. Ibid., pp. 34, 41.

53. Ibid., Forwarding statement, page unnumbered.

54. The New York Times, February 3, 1981, p. B-13.

55. The Washington Post, February 7, 1981, p. 10.

56. The New York Times, February 3, 1981, p. B-13.

57. Ibid.

58. Ernest Evans, Calling a Truce to Terrorism (Westport, CT: Greenwood Press, 1979), pp. 63-77. This book provides an excellent discussion of deterrence theory in relation to terrorism.

6
The Need for Organizational Response

    In responding to the need to maintain security for
its people, the U.S. government has attempted to come to
grips with the problem of terrorism. There are several
aspects of the phenomenon that make this task difficult.
Terrorism is not a constant; it waxes and wanes. Often
the characteristics of a terrorist act are idiosyncrat-
ic, taking on the peculiarities of a particular group,
geographic area, or manner of execution. The people of a
nation deserve protection and demand it when it is found
lacking. Yet, an action by the government that is effective in countering hijacking may have no effect on
reducing the incidents of bombing or kidnapping. The
government must respond to the many aspects of a problem contained under the one label -- terrorism.
    To better discern the nature of the terrorist threat,
it is worthwhile examining relevant statistical data.[1]
Of the 626 terrorist incidents recorded in North America
during the period January 1, 1970 through December 31,
1979, 618 occurred in the U.S. and only eight in Canada.
Within this ten year period, approximately sixty groups
were involved in the incidents -- all of which operated
in the United States (with the exception of one, the
Quebec Liberation Front).
    A very significant aspect of terrorist operations
in the United States is the substantial decline in activity over the 1976-79 period when compared to Latin America
and Europe. While these areas showed a rapid increase,
i.e., of 2234 operations recorded in Latin America between
1970 and 1979, seventy-six percent occurred in the last
four years. In Europe, of the 3562 terrorist incidents
reported during that time span, seventy-eight percent
took place in the last four years. For the United States,
the situation was reversed with only thirty-seven percent
taking place within the 1976-79 time frame. Terrorist
activity appears to have peaked prior to 1976 in the
United States, while the trend in other areas is still
climbing. Summary data for North America terrorist

activity for the decade of the 1970s are reflected in
Table 6.1.

The capabilities of terrorist groups can be judged
by the nature and type of operations undertaken as well
as the success rates recorded. By this standard, groups
involved almost exclusively in bombing (the least complex of all terrorist acts) could be considered less
sophisticated than those who devote substantial effort
to more complex actions (kidnapping, assassination, embassy attacks) and show a high success rate.[2] Measured
by these standards, United States terrorist organizations are much less effective than their Latin American
or European counterparts. In Latin America approximately
forty percent of all group actions were bombings while
the figure was approximately eighty-five percent for the
United States.

A primary target of all terrorist activity in the
United States has been businesses, mainly American firms.
However, since 1976 there has been a slight drop in business targeting. This has been attributed to a decline
in actions by Marxist-oriented groups, which have trad-
itionally attacked business, and a rise in activity by
anti-Castro Cuban elements, Puerto Rican nationalists,
and other radical groups such as the Jewish Defense
League which often operate against nonbusiness installations. Tables 6.2 through 6.6 provide a detailed analysis
of terrorist activity by type (i.e., assassinations, kidnappings, bombings, facility attacks, and hijackings).

The scope and variety of terrorist organizations
based in the United States have made the government's
response difficult. The past decade has seen radical
Marxist and prison-related groups such as the Weather
Underground, New World Liberation Front, Sam Melville-
Jonathan Jackson Unit, Revolutionary Communist Party,
George Jackson Brigade, Symbionese Liberation Army,
Black Panther Party, Red Guerrilla Family, and the Black
Guerrilla Family. There have been ethnic national
groups such as the Jewish Defense League, Croatians,
Serbians, and Armenians. Noteworthy among the nationalists
of late have been the Puerto Ricans (Armed Forces of National Liberation, Independent Armed Revolutionary Commandos) and the Cubans (Omega 7, Cuban National Liberation Front). The sudden influx of Cuban refugees during
the first half of 1980 may provide fertile grounds for
recruiting sympathetic soldiers to fill out the ranks
of Cuban groups.

In addition to the activity of indigenous groups,
foreign-based organizations also have conducted operations within the United States. Beyond the activity of
the Croatian and Armenian exile groups, both the Palestinian Black September Organization (BSO) and the Irish
Republican Army (IRA) have been operative. During March

TABLE 6.1

Terrorist Activity in North America, 1970-1979

	Worldwide 1970-1979	North America 1970-1979
Total Terrorist Incidents (all types)	8114	626
Number killed[1]	4987	73
Incidents Targeting U.S. Business	737	274
Total Dollar Losses[2]	$575,620,002	$16,015,810

North America, for purposes of this assessment, covers only Canada and the continental United States.

1. Accurate death/injury data and dollar losses are available in a very limited number of cases. Only verified data are reported here. Accordingly, the actual death/injury count and dollar loss figures undoubtedly are much higher.

2. Includes ransoms paid in kidnappings and hijackings; damage to plants, facilities, equipment and aircraft in bombings, facility attacks and hijackings; and funds taken in robberies.

Source: Regional Risk Assessment, North America, Risks International, Inc. (Alexandria, VA: 1979), p. 1. Executive Risk Assessment, "A Review of Terrorist Activity in 1979," Vol. 1, No. 12, 1979, same author, pp. 1-3.

TABLE 6.2

Assassinations, 1970-1979

	Worldwide 1970-1979	North America 1970-1979
Total Incidents	1233	48
Number of Victims	1410	35
Incidents Targeting U.S. Business	27	1

Source: Regional Risk Assessment, North America, Risks International, Inc. (Alexandria, VA: 1979), p. 3. Executive Risk Assessment, "A Review of Terrorist Activity in 1979" Vol. 1, No. 12, 1969, same author, pp. 1-8.

TABLE 6.3

Kidnappings, 1970-1979

	Worldwide 1970-1979	North America 1970-1979
Total Incidents	536	15
Victims Killed	84	1
Incidents Targeting U.S. Business	45	1
Ransoms Demanded[1]	$374,595,500	$1,230,000
Ransoms Paid[1]	$152,000,400	$ 700,000

---

1. Ransoms demanded and paid are those reported publicly. The listed dollar figures encompass only fifty percent of all kidnap incidents. Accordingly, the actual ransom demands and payments would be much higher.

Source: Regional Risk Assessment, North America, Risks International, Inc. (Alexandria, VA: 1979), p. 4. Executive Risk Assessment, "A Review of Terrorist Activity in 1979," Vol. 1, No. 12, 1979, same author, pp. 2-5.

TABLE 6.4

Bombings, 1970-1979

	Worldwide 1970-1979	North America 1970-1979
Total Incidents[1]	4407	531
Number Killed[2]	904	29
Number Injured[2]	4816	221
Incidents Targeting U.S. Business	501	249
Total Losses[2]	$146,219,440	$13,723,810
U.S. Business Losses	$ 25,691,670	$ 3,020,050

1. These do not include all terrorist bombings worldwide. Only those bombings were recorded where: (1) substantial human or material damage was done, (2) the target was unique, (3) the device was unusual, or (4) the method of emplacement was unusual.

2. Accurate death/injury data and those relating to dollar losses are available in a very limited number of cases. Only verifiable data are listed. Accordingly, the actual death/injured count and that relating to dollar damage are undoubtedly much higher.

Source: Regional Risk Assessment, North America, Risks International, Inc. (Alexandria, VA: 1979), p. 5. Executive Risk Assessment, "A Review of Terrorist Activity in 1979," Vol. 1, No. 12, 1979, same author, pp. 2-6.

TABLE 6.5

Hijackings,[1] 1970-1979

	Worldwide 1970-1979	North America 1970-1979
Total Incidents	89	5
Number Killed	60	--
Number Injured	42	--
Incidents Targeting U.S. Business	5	3
U.S. Ransoms Paid	$1,500,000	$1,500,000

1. Includes all hijackings, not simply those of air-craft. Trucks, buses, trains and ships also have been involved. These do not include criminal operations, those by demented individuals or those by political radicals unaffiliated with an organized terrorist group.

Source: Regional Risk Assessment, North America, Risks International, Inc. (Alexandria, VA: 1979), p. 7. Executive Risk Assessment, "A Review of Terrorist Activity in 1979," Vol. 1, No. 12, 1979, same author, pp. 2-8.

TABLE 6.6

Facility Attacks, 1970-1979

	Worldwide 1970-1979	North America 1970-1979
Total Incidents	1742	34
Number Killed[1]	2529	11
Number Injured[1]	1934	7
Incidents Targeting U.S. Business	78	19
Total Damages[1]	$166,228,100	$33,000
Total U.S. Business Damages	$ 17,457,500	$ 1,000

1. Accurate death/injury data and dollar damage/robbery loss information are available in less than ten percent of all reported cases. Only these verifiable data are listed. Accordingly, the actual death/injury counts and dollar damage/loss figures are much higher. Damages refer to physical injury to a facility.

Source: Regional Risk Assessment, North America, Risks International, Inc. (Alexandria, VA: 1979), p. 6. Executive Risk Assessment, "A Review of Terrorist Activity in 1979," Vol. 1, No. 12, 1979, same author, pp. 2-7.

6-7, 1973, the BSO placed three car bombs in areas of
New York City. The devices were placed near the El Al
freight terminal at Kennedy Airport, the Israeli Discount
Bank in Manhattan, and another nearby financial institution.
Each device contained one and one-half pounds of plastic
explosive, a twenty pound charged butane tank, and a five-
gallon can of gasoline. Fortunately, the timing mechanisms
failed in all three cases. It was estimated that, if the
bombs had gone off, there would have been a total loss of
life within one hundred yards of each blast point. The
BSO also assassinated the Israeli Attache, Colonel Yosef
Alon, in Washington on July 1, 1973. The IRA, in August
1973, mailed a letter bomb to the British Military Attache
in Washington. The device detonated in his office,
seriously injuring a secretary.

During 1975 and 1976 two associates of the Japanese
Red Army were arrested in Canada as they sought entry into
the United States. In July 1978 a West German terrorist
was arrested while crossing the U.S. - Canadian border
at Albury, Vermont.

A recent CIA study of international terrorism pre-
dicts more sophisticated attacks and foresees a global
rise in casualties because terrorists "may believe that
a larger number of casualties are now necessary to gener-
ate the amount of publicity formerly evoked by less
bloody operations." According to the study, a sizeable
portion of the terrorist incidents during 1979 occurred
in the industrialized countries of Western Europe and
North America. Many of the incidents were the work of
organizations from outside the region that had "chosen
to export their grievances."[3]

Using the statistical base for which data has been
presented in the study, the twelve months of 1979 were
the most active period of the decade. While a meager
total of 293 incidents for all of 1970 were reported,
there has been a steady increase ever since; in 1974 -
388 incidents; 1976 - 728; 1978 - 1,511. The total for
1979 is a staggering 2,585 incidents.[4] (See Table 6.7).
Only 111 of 2,585 incidents for 1979 involved U.S. installations or personnel. There were fifty-one acts
directed at U.S. corporations which equates to a little
less than two percent of the worldwide incident total.[5]

> Viewed geographically, 955 (37%) of the 2,585
> operations worldwide occurred in Europe, 877
> (33.9%) in Latin America, 144 (5.6%) in Asia,
> 466 (18.0%) in Sub-Saharan Africa and 36 (1.4%)
> in North America. As might be expected from
> the above figures, the greatest dollar damages
> were recorded in Europe and Latin America. . .
> In looking at the various world regions from
> the standpoint of terrorist acts directed

TABLE 6.7

Terrorist Activity for 1979

Type of Incident	Total	# Killed	#Injured	# U.S. Killed	# U.S. Injured
Kidnapping	132	34	0	2	0
Bombing	1069	227	1282	3	21
Facility Attacks	790	1084	889	20	15
Assassination	546	615	0	9	0
Maiming*	37	0	39	0	0
Hijacking	11	3	0	0	0
TOTAL	2585	1963	2210	34	36

*Maiming was not previously part of Risks published data. During 1979 this activity was confined to Italy, Northern Ireland and Spain.

Source: Executive Risk Assessment, "A Review of Terrorist Activity in 1979," Risks International, Inc., 1979, Vol. 1, No. 12, p. 2.

against U.S. personnel and facilities, the
most active area was Latin America. That
region alone accounted for 45 (40.5%) of
the 111 operations targeting U.S. interests
during 1979.[6]

Within the United States, during 1979 there were thirty-
one bombings, one kidnapping, two assassinations and two
hijackings.[7]
    Entering the decade of the 1980s one saw no let up
in terrorism. (See Table 6.8.) A record total of 2773
terrorist incidents were noted in 1980 -- up 188 from
1979. Over fifty percent took place in Latin America,
with a majority of those in just three nations: El
Salvador, Guatemala, and Columbia. The 2773 incidents
resulted in 4843 persons being killed (an increase of
almost 3000 compared to 1979). The number of injured
rose from 1171 to 3381. There was also an increase in
total material losses (from bombings, facility attacks,
and paid ransoms) of $72 million, to a total of
$148,767,040. Despite the relatively small increase
in incident numbers (188), the cost in lives and material
was substantial.
    Targeting of business continued to be a priority
item for terrorists, comprising thirty-one percent of
the 1980 total. This represented a slight decline from
1979 (1.8 percent). U.S. business interests were targeted 4.9 percent of the time, also reflecting a slight
drop, one percent, from 1979. Business targets accounted
for almost half of all the kidnapping and bombing attacks
recorded in 1980. U.S. business, as a result, saw two
employees killed and twenty-six injured. Four other
U.S. businessmen were killed in assassination actions
and four employees of American firms were killed in
facility attacks. In all, the total U.S. business losses
in terrorist activity relating to kidnapping, bombings,
and facility attacks approached $2.5 million. In contrast
to the frequency of business targets, government personnel
and installations were objects of terrorist attacks less
than twenty percent of the time. The police and military
comprised another twenty percent of terrorist targets.
    The first half of 1981 witnessed 1209 terrorist
incidents worldwide versus 1372 for the same period for
1980. Business targets dropped from a position as the
leading terrorist objective and was replaced by police
and military personnel or installations. This appears
to be attributable to the accelerated terrorist activity
in El Salvador, Guatemala, Columbia, and Spain. Each
of these nations had a well organized terrorist/guerilla
group engaged in direct attacks upon incumbent governments
and their police and military forces.[8]

TABLE 6.8

Terrorist Activity for 1980

Type of Incident	Total	# Killed	# Injured	# U.S. Killed	# U.S. Injured
Kidnapping	124	54	Unknown	2	0
Bombing	1006	528	2385	0	26
Facility Attacks	768	2415	977	5	7
Assassination	843	1846	Unknown	12	0
Maiming	18	0	19	0	0
Hijacking	14	0	0	0	0
TOTAL	2773	4843	3381	19	33

Source: Quarterly Risk Assessment, January-March 1981, Risks International, Inc., 1979, p. 47.

It had been predicted that businesses would involve
the largest single target category hit by terrorist
groups worldwide in the 1980s. Further, since U.S. firms
were targeted 1.9 percent in 1979, only to see this rise
to 4.9 percent for 1980, and 6.8 percent in just the
final quarter of that year, it was expected that these
businesses would continue to be hit with greater frequency. While the trend concerning business as a whole
has slowed slightly (based upon the statistics for the
first half of 1981), U.S. firms remain at approximately
the 1980 percentages.

Keeping in mind the current nature of terrorism in
Central and South America, it should be recalled that
the greatest risk to business does not occur during an
all out terrorist/guerilla offensive but rather in the
period in which the terrorist groups are building their
force or in the period following a failed offensive
when terrorists must revert to a rebuilding process. As
terrorists become more sophisticated and disciplined,
tactics and targets begin to change. Facility attacks
become more common, usually carried out by teams of five
or six and involving some automatic weapons. Police,
military, and government targets bear the brunt of the
attacks. When this occurs, operations involving bombing
of business offices or the abduction of corporate
personnel begin to decline.

The greatest risks to business from terrorist
operations are abductions for ransom and the bombing
of installations. Whether in Latin America, Europe,
Middle East, North Africa, or Asia, terrorists appear
to fully comprehend that business firms will almost
always pay ransom for abducted personnel. This policy
is very different from the usual government practice
which rarely allows such payments. Revenue obtained in
such abductions is a prime source of terrorist operational
funds.

Business establishments also remain a favored bombing
target, accounting for over fifty percent of all terrorist
bombings during 1980. The reason for this is not difficult
to determine. Police, military, and government facilities
can readily construct strict screening procedures in high
risk areas. Businesses cannot easily do likewise since
they depend on easy access for customers and investors.
Any curtailment of access could force them into financial ruin. Terrorists are well aware of this and have
acted accordingly.

During the latter half of 1979 and throughout all
of 1980 there was increasing emphasis by terrorists on
targets such as electrical power and telephone systems.
Interest in these facilities seems to be based upon the
notion that the knocking out of electrical grids, communications, and other essential utilities will reduce govern-

ment effectiveness, hinder commerce and business, and reduce public confidence in the government, thereby driving the people to the cause of the terrorist.

Whatever the ebbs and flows of statistical charts may indicate from year to year, the long term evidence is very clear: business will remain a significant terrorist target in the decade of the 1980s.

One of the many stimulii causing governmental concern with terrorism is the range of weapons available for carrying out terrorist activities. Increased technological sophistication can influence the nature of the target as well as the mode used to strike it. The following is a menu of weapons from which the modern day terrorist may choose:[9]

Bombs: There are two general classes available: explosive and incendiary. Explosive types are either fragmentation or blast devices. Fire bombs, which can be cheaply constructed, are easy to use and capable of inflicting a great deal of damage. Both types are extensively used by terrorists at home and abroad. They vary in sophistication from time-delay, fused, and pressure bombs to primitive mixtures of fertilizer and fuel oils. What makes the use of bombs an attractive option is that they allow the terrorist to be far removed from the scene when the damage is inflicted.

Automatic Weapons: These weapons are used by terrorists because they are easily concealed, fire rapidly, and impact greatly on lightly armed security forces. One drawback is that the arc-shaped or long rectangular magazines used in these weapons leave a distinctive signature when x-rayed.

Precision-Guided Munitions (PGMs): PGMs are capable of launching missiles whose trajectories can be corrected in flight. Many varieties are employable by one or two person teams. A Soviet version PGM, the SA-7, is believed to have been employed in Africa and Europe. It has been reported that thirty to forty Third World countries will possess these kinds of weapons in the 1980s. If a conservative rate of loss by theft or diversion is calculated (one tenth of one percent over a five year period) then hundreds of PGMs will be readily available for terrorist use.

Nuclear Devices: There is a great deal of speculation concerning the potential use of nuclear devices by terrorists. To date it has remained a matter of conjecture, but very frightening never the less. A terrorist need not bring forth a sleek, technically mature bomb, rather a crude device capable of exploding and causing some

damage is all that is needed. Yet the barriers to construction remain formidable, the material is dangerous
(deadly) to handle, difficult to work with, and requires
engineering skills possessed by relatively few. But
fear of nuclear blackmail is ever present, and could be
used by terrorists to their advantage.

Chemical and Biological Weapons: The spectre of
poisonous chemicals or dangerous bacteria felling
thousands of people is awesome. While machine guns
and fire bombs can cause several deaths at one time,
chemical and biological agents rival nuclear devices
in their killing capacity.

It is difficult to forecast the extent to which
terrorist groups would go to fulfill their objectives.
The Red Brigade of Italy would probably not choose to
employ weapons of mass destruction to make a point,
when kidnapping or assassination would be quite effective.
However, state sponsored terrorism of the Lybian variety
may well employ this tactic against an "imperialist
devil" such as the United States.
Of all the categories of weapons mentioned above,
the one that causes the greatest fear is the nuclear
device. This is a complex issue however, and needs to
be addressed briefly in any work on terrorism.
In July 1975 a nuclear extortion threat was made
against New York City. A group or individual conveyed
the following message:

> We have successfully designed and built an atomic
> bomb. It is somewhere on Manhattan Island. We
> refer you to the accompanying drawing in one-
> eighth scale. We have enough plutonium and
> explosives for the bomb to function. This device
> will be used at 6:00 p.m., July 10, unless our
> demands are met. Do not notify the public.
> This will result in hysteria and the use of the
> bomb.[10]

The author(s) sought $30 million in small bills. What
made the threat a grave matter of concern was the drawing
accompanying it. It was very precise and clearly made
by someone who had more than passing acquaintance with
nuclear physics. Responding to additional orders in the
message, the FBI inserted an announcement about a truck
incident in Vermont on the radio as a signal to the
extortionist that the demands were met. A dummy package
was placed at a specified drop site but no one ever
claimed it and nothing else ever developed.
This threat to New York was one of four such threats
to the city during the 1970s and one of sixty leveled

against other American cities and institutions during
that same period. No threat to date has been carried
through, but in an era when The Progressive magazine
has successfully won the right to publish a description
of a hydrogen bomb and a Princeton junior has made a
diagram of an atomic bomb, one can wonder if the day is
far off when a device will be present to back up the
threat.

Concern about terrorist threats going nuclear
center on two main areas: the seizing or sabotage of
a nuclear facility or the acquisition of material and
subsequent construction of a nuclear device. Some
scientists feel that it is no longer a matter of if,
but rather when such an act would be carried out.

Nuclear facilities have been the target of attacks
ranging from shooting at guards to the placement of
explosives at the site. Additionally, there have been
significant amounts of nuclear fuel materials discovered
missing (more than fifty tons) at the thirty four
uranium and plutonium processing plants in the country.
It has been estimated that between 6,000 and 7,000 pounds
of this is bomb grade material.[11] While the loss could
be attributible to accounting deficiencies, it is also
possible that some of it may have been deliberately
diverted for unauthorized use. The continued increase
in the numbers of nations that possess some form of
nuclear facility also gives valid cause for concern.

One target that at first may appear alluring for
theft or sabotage is a nuclear weapon. Despite the
dramatic scenario that could be imagined, there are some
major hinderances to any such attempt. The facilities
at which they are kept are heavily guarded by manpower
as well as sophisticated electronic devices. Further,
such nuclear weapons have internal nuclear security
systems which prevent the device from exploding pre-
maturely or from being disassembled to remove the nuclear
material. A more likely scenario would be the supplying
of a nuclear weapon to a terrorist group by a radical
nation state.

Aside from obtaining an existing weapon, the entire
fuel cycle process provides opportunities of which a
terrorist can take advantage. The theft of fissionable
material (weapons grade which can be readily used) is
seen as very remote. None of the commercial reactors
utilize such material. It is only found at the highly
protected weapons fabrication points. The most vulnerable
area seems to be during the reactor fuel cycle. But even
then the barriers are formidable and would require skill,
technical and scientific knowledge, and a good deal of
inside help. The weakest link appears to be in the
transportation mode when the material is being transferred
among facilities. One must recall that the terrorist

need not make a bomb to carry out his plan. The fear
generated by knowledge that a group possesses a transport
vehicle loaded with nuclear material capable of causing
widespread radiation may be all that is needed to extract
demands.[12]

In addition to the terrorism itself, governmental
agencies are affected in the scope and nature of their
response by additional outside forces. Two of these,
the Congress and the president, will be briefly examined.

The Role of Congress

While Congress has conducted several hearings
concerning various aspects of both terrorism and counter-
terrorism, perhaps the most significant centered upon
Senate Bill 2236.[13] This bill was directed at strength-
ening federal policies and programs as well as international cooperative efforts to combat terrorism. Work on
the bill began in 1977 and hearings were conducted during the early months of 1978. It represented the culmin-
ation of a six-month examination by the Senate Governmental Affairs Committee of terrorist activity throughout the past decade and the policy problems inherent in
any strategy for its control. The scope of the committee's
activity was quite large as it

> . . . . .studied the crisis management needs of
> the United States in coping with a sizeable ter-
> rorist incident, the potential organizational,
> legal, and jurisdictional problems involving Fed-
> eral, State, and local authorities in such situ-
> ations, the adequacy and effectiveness of multi-
> lateral treaties in this field, problems rela-
> ting to the need for and development of a mili-
> tary capability in domestic and international
> terrorist incidents, the structure, organiza-
> tion, financing, weaponry, strategy, and tac-
> tics of various international terrorist groups,
> the extent of effective minimum security stan-
> dards at foreign airports serving the United
> States, the level and effectiveness of physical
> and personal security at U.S. diplomatic and
> military installations abroad, and finally the
> extent and effectiveness of U.S. intelligence
> reporting on terrorist activity and terrorist
> access to and misuse of explosive materials.[14]

One of the publicly proferred reasons put forth by the
committee for undertaking its review was that the executive branch had not assigned a high enough priority to
U.S. policy for combating terrorism. The executive pol-
icy-making apparatus was viewed as needing to more

effectively define its goals, develop alternative initiatives in both bilateral and multilateral contexts and to better integrate the concerns and objectives of antiterrorism policy. Within the executive branch, few officials saw a significant threat of terrorism to the United States and believed that any situation could be handled if the need arose.[15]

S2236, as introduced, provided for a reorganization of the government's structure for combating terrorism. The changes would have centered on the creation of a new post of assistant secretary in the State Department to head the Office for Combating Terrorism; creation of a new post of Assistant Attorney General and a special office in the Department of Justice to handle its efforts in this regard; and, lastly, creation of a permanent Council for Combating Terrorism in the executive office of the president to coordinate the government's handling of a major terrorist incident.[16] This council was to be headed by the Assistant to the President for National Security Affairs and was to serve as the lead group in establishing procedures to insure that the U.S. could take action in response to acts of terrorism. The council would coordinate and evaluate all such programs undertaken by government agencies.[17]

Secretary of State Cyrus Vance had argued before the committee against the recommended organizational changes. He stated that the federal mechanisms in operation were sufficient as a result of PRM 30 and that S2236 would only lead to duplication.[18]

Since the reorganization of the executive department was apparently being undertaken (PRM 30) at the same time as Congress was about to propose changes, the committee amended the bill -- deleting the need for structural changes. In lieu of this, the committee would require a comprehensive report of federal capabilities to combat terrorism. Within six months after the date of enactment, and at intervals of two years, the president was to submit to Congress a report containing a comprehensive and specific review of federal antiterrorism organization, policies, and activities. The report was to also include descriptions of structures, planning, coordination (including with state and local authorities), response capability and intelligence-gathering and analysis.[19]

In the conduct of interviews with members of Congressional staffs, additional relevant data concerning the Senate bill was discovered.[20] It was strongly suggested that the bill was never really intended to legislate organizational change. The bill's primary purpose was to signal to the world that the U.S. was determined to do something to meet the problems posed by terrorism. Senator Abraham Ribicoff, Chairman of the Committee on Governmental Affairs, was deeply concerned with the need

to take action. A close friend, Senator Jacob Javits,
was likewise concerned and the two agreed to press the
issue in Congress. For Senator Ribicoff to have a clear
say in the process, part of the bill would have to center
on government reorganization and thus come before his
committee. The bill also contained provisions relating
to international agreements (e.g., aviation safety), and,
when it was reviewed by the Foreign Relations Committee,
all organization material was removed. This did not come
as a surprise to those on Ribicoff's staff: it was
fully expected. Further, since the executive branch
had completed PRM 30, it was decided to allow its organization change to take place without Congress' putting
in its two cents' worth. However, the requirement for
the president to report on counterterrorist activity
was retained to indicate Congress' continuing interest
in the problem.

The future of the bill is a matter of speculation.
It contains provisions concerning explosives, aviation,
and international agreements sparking the interest of
several committees and interest groups. With "many other
priorities" in an election year, passage in 1980 did not
come about.

In 1974, Congress enacted Public Law 93-366 which
was composed of the Antihijacking Act and the Air Transportation Security Act. This law gave the Federal Aviation Administration exclusive responsibility for the direction of any law enforcement activity affecting the safety of persons aboard aircraft. In flight was to be the
time from the moment when external doors are closed following embarkation until the moment when one such door is
opened for disembarkation. The law also authorized the
agency to establish and arm a law enforcement section to
carry out the provisions of the act.[21]

One additional act passed by Congress affecting governmental response to terrorism was Public Law 94-467, an
"Act for the Prevention and Punishment of Crimes Against
Internationally Protected Persons." This act makes it a
federal crime to, "among other things, murder, assault,
threaten, extort, kidnap or offer violence to a foreign
official, official guest or internationally protected
person or to his official premises, private accommodations
or means of transportation." If the victim of an offense
under this act is such a protected person and the suspect
is in the United States, the U.S. may "exercise jurisdiction over the offense regardless of where the offense was
committed or the nationality of the victim or alleged
offender."[22]

The role of Congress relative to countering terrorism is expected to be substantial through at least the
early 1980s. Not only will the various committees dealing
with foreign relations be concerned, since the number

one foreign policy goal of the Reagan administration is
now thwarting international terrorism, but also, the Senate has established a permanent subcommittee on terrorism
and subversion.

The Role of the President

The influence of the president can be viewed from
two perspectives: direction to the executive agencies
to perform certain acts and personal involvement in
a particular incident as it unfolds.

Two clear examples, since 1972, of presidential direction of organizational change occurred in the Nixon
and Carter administrations. As set forth in Chapter 4,
because of the 1972 Munich massacres, President Nixon
established the Cabinet Committee to Combat Terrorism in
order to coordinate the policy planning of the federal
government's program for dealing with the threat. "In
the five years of its existence, the committee accomplished
little towards filling its mandate."[23] Because of the
committee's inactivity, President Carter abolished it in
late 1977. Pursuant to Presidential Review Memorandum
30, the federal government's response was reorganized
under the aegis of the Special Coordination Committee
(SCC) of the National Security Council. "Only in the
event of a major incident, requiring the highest level
of decision-making, will the SCC become involved."[24]

The president, by virtue of his position, has the
ability to become involved in any foreign or domestic
issue which he chooses. He can manipulate the decision
making process, set the tone by formal or informal lines
of authority, and encourage diversity or consensus.[25]
Since terrorist incidents take on a sense of crisis, it
is to be expected that the "critical decisions will
continue to be made by the president and his principal
advisors."[26]

> A crisis situation presents the President with
> an unusual opportunity to lead the policy pro-
> cess; he can define the crisis, initiate organ-
> izational and interdepartmental procedures for
> crisis management, set deadlines, and generally
> guide the process of decision making . . . . .
> The media, the Congress, interest groups, and
> the public have relatively less effect on the
> crisis decision-making process because of their
> lack of information and the pace of events.[27]

One situation occurring March 1, 1973, can be illus-
trative of presidential intervention in a terrorist incident. On that date in the Sudan, eight members of the
Black September Organization took over the Saudi Arabian

Embassy in Khartoum during a party. They seized several
hostages, including U.S. Ambassador Cleo A. Noel, U.S. Deputy Chief of Mission George Moore, and Belgian Chargé Guy
Eid. The terrorists demanded the release of sixty Palestinian guerrillas being held in Jordan, all Arab women
detained in Israel, Sirhan Sirhan, and members of the
Baader-Meinhof Gang imprisoned in Germany. Negotiations
were undertaken by the Sudanese government, and the
terrorists dropped their demands on Israeli and West
German governments.[28]

On March 2, 1973, during a news conference, President
Nixon was asked the following question:

> Mr. President, we have a crisis, of course,
> in the Sudan, where the U.S. Ambassador is
> being held hostage and one of the ransom
> demands is that Sirhan Sirhan be released.
> I wonder if you have any comment on this,
> particularly on that demand.
>
> The President:. . . As far as the United States
> as a government giving in to blackmail demands,
> we cannot do so and we will not do so. Now, as
> to what can be done to get these people released,
> Mr. Macomber (William B. Macomer, Jr., Deputy
> Undersecretary of State for Management) is on
> his way there for discussions. The Sudanese
> Government is working on the problem. We will
> do everything that we can to get them released,
> but we will not pay blackmail.[29]

On the evening of March 2, the terrorists executed the
two U.S. diplomats and the Belgian Chargé.[30] It has
been suggested that the terrorists, who were in radio
contact with some form of Palestinian command center,
killed the three as a result of believing that negotiations with the U.S. had been foreclosed by the president's
statement. Additionally, Macomber had taken charge of the
task force at the State Department handling the incident.
While traveling to the Sudan he retained that authority
which meant that for approximately fifteen hours, while
Macomber was en route, no one at the command center was
authorized to act in his stead. Macomber was still
traveling when the three were killed.[31]

On March 6, 1973, President Nixon commented:

> All of us would have liked to have saved the
> lives of these two very brave men, but they
> knew and we knew that in the event we paid
> international blackmail in this way, it would
> have saved their lives but it would have
> endangered the lives of hundreds of others

> all over the world, because once the
> individual, the terrorist, or others (sic)
> has a demand that is made, that is satisfied,
> he is encouraged to try it again, and that is
> why the position of your government has to be
> one in the interest of preserving life, of not
> submitting to international blackmail or ex-
> tortion anyplace in the world.[32]

This policy of no concessions was to remain the publicly stated stand taken by the U.S. through the Carter
administration. It was a part of the deterrence strategy
to decrease terrorist incidents and "save human lives not
only in the long run but in the short run as well."[33]
    Secretary of State Kissinger stated on occasion that,
if terrorists receive the impression that they can force
acquiescence, then lives saved at one place would risk
lives elsewhere. It was acknowledged that such a policy
was heartbreaking in individual cases but deemed necessary to deter the kidnapping of Americans.[34] In the
aftermath of the Croatian nationalist hijacking of a
TWA airliner from New York to Paris in September 1976
and again in 1978, it was clearly stated that the "U.S.
will make no concessions to terrorist blackmail."[35]
    Evaluating the American policy of refusing all con-
cessions has not been easy. Recalling what was set forth
in Chapter 2, defining terrorism was a difficult task
because such acts could be undertaken for several purposes.
If the terrorist's primary goal was increased publicity
or the creation of fear rather than the receiving of ransom, the deterrent effect of no concession would be limited indeed. "In light of the questionable benefits and
real costs of the current American policy toward hostage
situations, there is a need to undertake a fundamental
reformulation of this policy."[36]
    During the Ford administration the Croatian hijacking
took place, but no public policy-setting statements
could be discovered. While the hijacking was significant,
it could be speculated that the death of Chairman Mao
and its effects on American policy may have monopolized
his time, lessening presidential desire to become involved.
    During March 1977 two incidents occurred which dem-
onstrated the potential for presidential involvement when
he deems it necessary. On March 8, President Carter
offered to become personally involved in a criminal
hostage case taking place in Warrensville Heights, Ohio.
While admitting that it was ". . . . perhaps a dangerous
precedent to establish, I weighed that factor before I
made my own decision."[37] After hearing that the president
would talk to him, the suspect released his hostage.

On March 9, 1978, several members of the Hanafi Moslems seized three buildings and 134 hostages in Washington, D.C., for what was to be, according to the U.S. Attorney for the District of Columbia, a thirty-eight-hour "reign of terror."[38] President Carter, apparently disestablishing the dangerous precedent set a few days before, did not become directly involved. Attorney General Griffin Bell and FBI Director Clarence Kelley went to the on-scene command post to evaluate the situation. The Attorney General then made what has been described as a "very astute political judgement"[39] and reported to the White House that enough agencies were already involved and that additional assistance from the chief executive was not needed at that time. The incident was successfully resolved through the combined efforts of several agencies and three Islamic ambassadors who acted as negotiators.

During a speech on January 27, 1981, President Reagan set the tone for his administration's response to terrorism. Addressing the former hostages of the Iranian ordeal he stated:

> Those henceforth in the representation of this nation will be accorded every means of protection that America can offer. Let terrorists be aware that when the rules of international behavior are violated, our policy will be swift and effective retribution.
>
> We hear it said that we live in an era of limit to our powers. Well, let it also be understood that there are limits to our patience.[40]

For those in the government directly concerned with the counterterror effort the fact that marching orders had been issued was quite clear. The tempo of the cadence and the exact direction of the march would be governed by the existing structures and routines of the organizations. Additionally, the very nature of terrorism and its multifaceted manifestations have caused organizations to undergo changes to meet the challenge. What follows is an examination of the effects upon select executive agencies as they attempted to counter terrorism.

NOTES

1. The author is extremely grateful to Mr. Roy Tucker, President of Risks International, Inc., Alexandria, Va., for access to the company's data base. The materials contained in the data base relate to significant actions carried out by terrorist groups operating

within the United States and overseas, <u>excluding</u> communist countries. Actions by criminal <u>elements</u> are <u>not</u> recorded. The information is derived from foreign and U.S. government reports, police reports and foreign/ English language press. Data relating to damages, persons killed and wounded, and hostages taken is dependent upon the accuracy of such reporting.

2. Activity such as kidnapping, assassination, and attacks on business or governmental facilities requires a relatively high degree of organizational sophistication. It requires that the group have an excellent intelligence-collection capability, an effective support organization and access to automatic weapons, vehicles and safe houses. These tactics are employed most frequently by disciplined and well-trained groups. It is interesting to note the influence of the media in this regard. Although terrorist kidnappings and assassinations in Italy have received more publicity than those of any other European nation, Spain leads the region in both categories. Between 1970-1978, thirty-five terrorist kidnappings were recorded in that country versus twenty-seven in Italy. More than twice as many assassinations have occurred in Spain as in Italy (136 versus 59).

3. Drew Middleton, "1979 Terrorist Toll Put at a Record 587," <u>The New York Times</u>, May 11, 1980, p. 14.

4. Risks International, Inc., "A Review of Terrorist Activity in 1979," <u>Executive Risk Assessment</u>, Volume 1, Number 12 (Alexandria, VA: 1979), p. 1.

5. <u>Ibid</u>.

6. <u>Ibid</u>., p. 3.

7. <u>Ibid</u>., pp. 3-4.

8. Risks International, Inc. provided the data for 1980-1981 upon which the above paragraphs are based.

9. Robert H. Kupperman, "The Threat: Some Technological Considerations" appearing in Yonah Alexander and Robert A. Kilmark <u>Political Terrorism and Business: The Threat and Response</u> (New York: Praeger Publishers, 1979), pp. 3-11.

10. Larry Collins, "Combating Nuclear Terrorism," <u>New York Times Magazine</u>, December 14, 1980, p. 36.

11. Richard H. Schultz, Jr., "The State of the Operational Art: A Critical Review of Anti-Terrorist Programs," <u>Responding to the Terrorist Threat</u>, Richard H. Schultz, Jr., and Stephen Sloan, eds. (New York: Pergamon Press, 1980), pp. 38-41.

12. <u>Ibid</u>.

13. Terrorism does not fall exclusively into any committee's area of jurisdiction. Consequently, congressional hearings relating to governmental affairs, foreign aid, aviation, intelligence, judicial matters, budgets, etc., have been held concerning the subject.

14. U.S. Congress, Senate, Committee on Governmental Affairs, An Act to Combat International Terrorism,
Report (Washington: U.S. Govt. Print. Off., 1978), pp.
1-2.

15. Ibid., p. 4.

16. Ibid., p. 45.

17. Draft of Senate Bill 333, 96th Congress, 1st
Session, February 5, 1979, titled Omnibus Antiterrorism
Act of 1979, p. 9. This is the same bill as S2236. Num-
erical change is due to carry-over into new legislative
year.

18. Cyrus R. Vance, "Statement," U.S. Congress,
Senate, Committee on Governmental Affairs, An Act to
Combat International Terrorism, Hearings (Washington:
U.S. Govt. Print. Off., 1978), pp. 8-11.

19. Senate Bill 333, pp. 17-18.

20. The following paragraphs are the result of
interviews conducted on February 22, February 24, and
February 25, 1980, with staff members of the Senate's
Governmental Affairs and Foreign Relations Committees
and the House's Judiciary Committee. The interviews
were granted on a nonattribution basis.

21. Public Law 93-366, 93rd Congress, S. 39,
August 5, 1974, Section 316 e 3.

22. An Act to Combat International Terrorism,
Report, p. 284.

23. U.S. Congress, House, Committee on the Jud-
iciary, Federal Capabilities in Crisis Management and
Terrorism, Staff Report (Washington: U.S. Govt. Print.
Off., 1979), p. 6.

24. Ibid., p. 7.

25. For an interesting discussion of this aspect
of presidential influence as it applied to Viet-Nam, see
Robert L. Gallucci, Neither Peace Nor Honor (Baltimore:
Johns Hopkins University Press, 1975).

26. Richard G. Head, et al., Crisis Resolution:
Presidential Decision Making in the Mayaguez and Korean
Confrontations (Boulder, CO: Westview Press, 1978),
p. 83.

27. Ibid., p. 221.

28. Brian M. Jenkins and Janera Johnson, International Terrorism: A Chronology, 1968-1974 (Santa Monica,
CA: The Rand Corporation, R-1597-DOS/ARPA, 1975), p. 39.

29. "President Nixon's Press Conference, March 2,
1973," Department of State Bulletin, March 26, 1973, p. 350.

30. Jenkins and Johnson, p. 39.

31. Interview with a former State Department
member who had continuing access to the command center
during the hostage incident, February 24, 1980.

32. "Remarks by President Nixon, March 6, 1973,"
Department of State Bulletin, March 26, 1973, p. 350.

33. Ernest Evans, <u>Calling a Truce to Terror</u>
(Westport, CT: Greenwood Press, 1979), p. 80.
34. "Secretary Kissinger's News Conference at
Vail, Colorado, August 17, 1975," <u>Department of State</u>
<u>Bulletin</u>, September 15, 1975, p. 408: "Secretary Kissin-
ger Appears Before Southern Governors Conference,"
Department of State Bulletin, October 6, 1975, p. 527.
35. "Policy of Refusal to Negotiate with Terrorists Reiterated," <u>Department of State Bulletin</u>, October
11, 1976, p. 453; "Terrorism: Scope of the Threat and
the Need for Effective Legislation," <u>Department of State</u>
<u>Bulletin</u>, March 1978, p. 54. It is interesting to note
that, in comparing data relating to terrorist kidnappings
of U.S., German, and Japanese individuals between 1970 and
1975, both Germany and Japan made concessions and neither
lost a life. Both are industrial "imperialist" countries
capable of meeting ransom demands, yet the total of hostage incidents directed against them (15) is less than
half of those (34) directed against the U.S. In twenty-
one of the American hostage situations the targets were
government personages and five were killed. In eleven
of the thirteen other cases, which were directed against
private individuals, the demands were completely met
from business or personal sources. (In the twelfth case
the company tried to pay the ransom but the local government seized the money. Whether or not a ransom was paid
in the thirteenth case is not known.) A CIA study published in August 1978 stated that, of the political
hostage situations in the seven-year period 1971-1977,
a "heavily disproportionate number (35%) involved
American nationals."
36. <u>Ibid</u>., p. 90. In fact, the U.S. has made
concessions in terrorist cases. During the Croatian hijacking of 1976, the terrorist demands for publication of
their demands and the dropping of leaflets were met. It
is the policy of the Federal Aviation Administration to
grant concessions in efforts to save lives. The FBI also
will allow concessions but in all cases it is made clear
that such concessions were minor, and a semantic exercise
ensues to illustrate how this is not a deviation from
official policy.
37. <u>New York Times</u>, March 10, 1977, p. 26.
38. <u>Ibid</u>., p. 18.
39. Interview with Robert H. Kupperman on January
22, 1980. Dr. Kupperman was formerly the Chief Scientist
for the U.S. Arms Control and Disarmament Agency and is
affiliated with the Georgetown Center for International
Studies, Washington, D.C. Apparently Attorney General
Bell realized that, if the situation went awry after
possible involvement by the White House, a trail of
dead bodies could lead to the president's door. Should

the agencies handling the crisis succeed, the president
would be in a position to praise those concerned.
    40. <u>New York Times</u>, January 28, 1981, p. A-14.

7
How the Organizations Responded

The senior-level Executive Committee on Terrorism
(ECT), which functioned up to the Reagan administration,
was composed of representatives from the departments of
State, Defense, Justice, Treasury, Transportation, and
Energy; the Central Intelligence Agency; and the National
Security Council staff. The new interagency group is
basically the same but added a representative from the
office of the vice president. In confronting terrorism
in the United States, each organization approached the
issue with an existing structure and methodology for
solving problems. Since terrorism represented either
a new area of concern or, at the minimum, a modified version of existing areas of responsibility, each organization had to undergo some degree of change. This chapter
seeks to examine the organizations identified above (with
the exception of that of the vice president, since it
only recently became a player) and determine how each
adjusted to this phenomenon. Such aspects as perceptions,
structures (formal and informal mechanics), weighting,
and vesting will be reviewed.

Department of State

The Department of State's involvement in countering
terrorism stems directly from President Nixon's establishment of the Cabinet Committee to Combat Terrorism on
September 22, 1972. Secretary William Rogers chaired
the Committee and a representative of the department was
to chair the Working Group established to assist the
Committee. Since the Cabinet Committee met only once,
the Working Group became the organ for coordinating the
counterterrorist policies.

The first chairman of the Working Group was Ambassador Armin H. Meyer. Within the department he became the
Special Assistant to the Secretary and Coordinator for
Combating Terrorism. Ambassador Meyer at the same time
was serving as Deputy Assistant Secretary for Near Eastern and South Asian Affairs. In the past he had been

envoy to Lebanon, Iran, and Japan.[1] His deputy, John A.
Gatch, was also experienced in Middle Eastern affairs.
It was the perception of the department that terrorism
was fundamentally a problem whose origin was in the Middle East.[2]

It is important to recognize that within State a
separate office or organization was not created at this
time. Rather, it was the position of Special Assistant
with a deputy. The actual Office for Combating Terrorism
was not established until the summer of 1976. At that
time the director of the office was no longer responsible
to the Secretary but instead came under the purview of
the Deputy Under Secretary for Management.[3]

Since the Working Group, as the support for the Cabinet Committee, was to bring "the full resources of all
appropriate U.S. agencies to bear effectively on the task
of eliminating terrorism wherever it occurs,"[4] it is il-
lustrative to examine how State as the chair agency
vested and weighted the office within the department.
While Meyer held his post as chairman of the Working
Group from October 1972, Gatch was not appointed as deputy until January 1973. It was not until March of that
year that a full-time secretary was assigned. Ambassador
Meyer retired on May 30, 1973 and was replaced on July 2
by Ambassador Lewis Hoffacker, who assumed the duties as
special assistant on a full-time basis. During the late
spring of 1973 a student from a local university was also
assigned as an intern. Hoffacker had previously served
as political advisor to the Commander in Chief, Atlantic
Fleet. In February 1975, Hoffacker retired and was replaced in April of that year by Robert Fearey. Fearey
came to the office after serving as chairman of the
Department of International Relations and Area Studies
at the National War College. Prior to that he had served
in the Pacific as political advisor to the Commander in
Chief and Civil Administrator for Okinawa.[5] Gatch retired in May 1975 and was replaced by Edward Schaefer,
who remained in his post until October of that same year.
Fearey transferred in July 1976, and was replaced by
L. Douglas Heck, the former ambassador to Niger. Schaefer's
replacement, Edward Hurwitz, stayed at the post of deputy
for less than a year, to be replaced in August 1976 by
John E. Karkashian. Heck, in June 1977, was named
ambassador to Nepal, and Karkashian was appointed acting
director until October 1977 when Heyward Isham, former
United States ambassador to the nation of Haiti, was
appointed. Isham remained at his post until July 1978,
when he was reassigned to the National War College. That
same month Anthony C. E. Quainton was designated as director
of the Office for Combating Terrorism. Quainton had previously been ambassador to the Central African Empire.

In reviewing this history of the effort by the department to counter terrorism, it must be noted that the individual to chair the Working Group had been changed seven times in as many years, 1972-1978. Those who left the post either retired or were assigned to relatively minor posts. Quainton seemed to reverse that trend and remained in his job from July 1978 through the summer of 1981. As the result of additional organizational change (November 1979), the director now carries the rank of ambassador and the office was placed under the Deputy Secretary of State.[6]

In discussions with individuals who either have functioned as staff members in State's terrorism office or had a continuing association with it as representatives of other departments within State or outside agencies dealing with terrorism, the organizational weight of the office became apparent. It was termed a dead-end assignment, graveyard, and a no-win situation.[7] Immediately after President Nixon's mandate in 1972 there was high-level interest, but this soon trailed off as matters became more routine. With the appointment of Ambassador Quainton and his "long" tenure in the post as director, this perception appears to have undergone some change. Several persons, in describing the importance of the office (as viewed from outside State), use the terms pre-Quainton and post-Quainton. His taking over, following the impetus for change flowing from PRM 30, gave new weight to the office. As one Senate staff assistant indicated, other agencies who had to deal with State did not miss how the terrorism office was viewed by its parent department. Cognizant of this, these other offices tended to treat it accordingly, giving it less weight than the situation itself (terrorism) rightfully demanded.[8] By the end of the 1970s, the Office for Combatting Terrorism had nine full-time employees, including three secretaries.

It was previously set forth in Chapter 5 that Quainton recognized that the number of participants in meetings of the Working Group was too large for effective policy coordination. Therefore, a reorganization along functional lines was undertaken. Two of those committees, the Security Policy Committee (Domestic) and Contingency Planning and Crisis Management (Foreign and Domestic), though now defunct, are relevant to the scope of this paper. The Security Policy Committee was co-chaired by the departments of Justice and Treasury. The domestic subcommittee of the Crisis Management Committee was chaired by Justice. The committees met infrequently in full session. The chairman felt it easier to deal with members on a one-to-one basis rather than as a functioning whole.[9]

With the arrival of Alexander M. Haig, Jr. as the Secretary of State under President Ronald Reagan, clear signals were broadcast to the world that terrorism would be an extremely sensitive topic. "International terrorism will take the place of human rights" as the priority concern of the administration.[10] During the summer of 1981 the Under Secretary for Management, Richard T. Kennedy, testified before the Senate Foreign Relations Committee that the Reagan administration had taken a "number of concrete steps to enhance our ability to prevent terrorist incidents and to manage those incidents which occur." Internally, in efforts to improve management and resource utilization the department developed still another organizational plan. The Office for Combating Terrorism is to report directly to Kennedy, which would mean that "planning and policy as reflected in the counterterrorism office, and the resources for response to threats represented in the security office, will both be under single jurisdiction." In such a way it was hoped that State would integrate its activities to enhance its ability to respond to a terrorist threat. But this structure is not too different from the organization in the 1976-1979 time frame when the office came under the Deputy Under Secretary for Management.[11] The melding of the Office to Combat Terrorism with those dealing with security will be interesting. The former is composed of foreign service officers where the latter is not. Both offices have different career patterns and world views.

The Department of Transportation

There are two agencies within the Department of Transportation which are primarily concerned with terrorism: the Federal Aviation Administration (FAA) and the U.S. Coast Guard (USCG). The FAA perceives the problem as one dealing with aviation safety while the USCG is concerned with maritime law enforcement.

Federal Aviation Administration: On September 6, 1970, a well-coordinated plan by the Popular Front for the Liberation of Palestine resulted in three hijackings of aircraft bound for New York from Europe and subsequent diversion of them to locations in the Middle East. Two of the carriers were American: Pan American and Trans-World Airlines, while the other was a Swissair DC-8. The PFLP announced that the hijackings were in retaliation for American support for Israel and the U.S. peace efforts in the Middle East. An attempted hijacking of an El Al plane was thwarted. On September 9, 1970, the PFLP hijacked a BOAC VC-10 and flew it to the Middle East, where the total number of hostages climbed to 300.[12]

As a direct result of these events, President Nixon announced on September 11, 1970, that sky marshals

would now be placed on international flights and the program would begin the following day.[13] While the September
incidents actually caused the Federal Sky Marshal program
to begin, it was also an effort to reverse the hijacking
trend that had begun in the late 1960s. Between 1960
and 1967 there had been only nine attempted or successful
hijackings on U.S. registered aircraft. During the years
1968 through 1972 the number had jumped to 134. From
1973 through 1979 the number fell considerably, totaling
only thirty-four. The FAA considers hijacking a criminal
act which is occasionally committed by a terrorist.
Terrorism is thus only a segment of a larger problem --
aviation safety.[14]

When the sky marshal program began it encompassed
people from several agencies, to include the Department
of Defense and the U.S. Customs Service (Department of
Treasury). In 1974, when the program was terminated,
security screening at airports was deemed sufficient to
eliminate the need for onboard marshals.

The successsful antihijacking effort continued until
July 1980, when there began a series of eleven hijackings
by Cuban refugees in the United States. FAA officials
were taken aback and immediately sought ways to remedy
the situation. An existing profile of a hijacker was reviewed and modified to meet the category of person currently deemed a threat. The airlines were provided with
the new profile and required to employ them in screening
passengers. It has been estimated that this technique
was successful in preventing seven additional attempted
hijackings. Premier Fidel Castro provided some additional
help by returning two hijackers to the U.S. for prosecution. FAA officials arranged for this fact to be well
publicized in areas of high density Cuban population.
It is believed that this and the profile abated the
problem for the time being.[15]

Additionally, in 1972, the Office of Civil Aviation
Security was established within the Office of the Secretary of Transportation. Retired Air Force Lieutenant
General Benjamin O. Davis was named as its first head.
He was subsequently named Assistant Secretary and the
office was headed by Richard Lally, the current director
of the Office of Aviation Security. The Office of Civil
Aviation Security is no longer in existence. It has been
replaced by the Office of Transportation Security which
concerns itself with all other modes of transportation,
excepting aircraft. This office is under the Research
and Special Programs Directorate and does not have the
weight or mandate of its predecessor.[16]

The FAA, with the cooperation of the FBI, has held
"incident management" exercises to fine-tune procedures
in hijacking cases. Additionally, both agencies have
trained flight crews and cabin attendants in procedures

to follow during these cases. Programs such as these did not come about as a result of the Executive Committee or the Working Group, but developed as a result of mutual concerns by the FAA and the FBI.

As indicated in Chapter 6, the FAA became more deeply involved in hijacking terrorist incidents as the result of the Antihijacking Act of 1974. Part II of the Act (known as the Air Transportation Security Act) confers upon the FAA the exclusive responsibility for the direction of any law enforcement activity affecting the safety of persons aboard aircraft involved in the commission or attempted commission of aircraft piracy and prohibits the transfer or assignment of those responsibilities. Other agencies are required, upon FAA request, to provide assistance. This law is the result of an extensive lobbying effort on the part of airline pilots who sought to have a sympathetic and knowledgeable agency directing law enforcement actions during the crucial period between embarkation and disembarkation. Pilots concerned primarily with aviation security sought to deal with an organization known to have a similar mind-set.[17]

United States Coast Guard: During peacetime the Coast Guard, while a branch of the Armed Forces, "is a service within the Department of Transportation."[18] Its functions relative to terrorism would center on maritime law enforcement, commercial vessel safety, and port safety and security. Since the demand for energy has spurred the rapid development of domestic assets on the continental shelf, the Coast Guard is becoming increasingly involved in countering possible terrorist attacks against such facilities. There are approximately 2,000 oil platforms and 12,000 miles of pipeline that could be the target of hostile groups. Additionally, attacks against vessels in port or within U.S. territorial waters are also a definite possibility. In 1979, a Memorandum of Understanding between the Director, Federal Bureau of Investigation, and the Commandant, United States Coast Guard, was signed concerning a policy of mutual assistance to counteract terrorist activities in a maritime environment. This brief two-page document recognized the unique capabilities of the two forces and the need for close coordination and cooperation to insure adequate response to terrorist activity. It was agreed that, subject to operational and budgetary constraints, the two agencies would provide mutual support and continue to plan to insure specific communications, command and control policy between Coast Guard Districts and FBI Regional Offices.[19]

Operational constraints such as narcotics control (antismuggling efforts), the demanding Cuban sealift, and the Haitian refugee problem have greatly taxed USCG resources. The Memorandum of Understanding between the

USCG and the FBI can be viewed as an "agreement to agree,"[20] and a recognition of the potential dangers posed by terror- ism. The USCG does not possess a special unit designated to neutralize a terrorist act. However, based upon a grant provided by the Law Enforcement Assistance Administration, the USCG undertook a wide-ranging study of the threat to maritime assets during 1980. This was to be followed by an attempt to educate members of the organization in this regard. What will then be needed is the convincing of the powers that be of the requirement of organization change and resource allocation. In a period of budget austerity this will be a formidable task indeed.[21]

Department of the Treasury

The Department does not view terrorism from primarily an economic perspective but rather from a law enforcement perspective. The responsibility falls under the purview of the Assistant Secretary for Enforcement and Operations. This office supervises the Secret Service, Customs Service, Federal Law Enforcement Training Center, and the Bureau of Alcohol, Tobacco and Firearms. The U.S. Secret Service's prime mission is the protecting of the president and the members of his immediate family, the president-elect, the vice president, the vice president-elect, major presidential and vice presidential candidates, former presidents and their wives and minor children, and the visiting heads of foreign states or foreign governments. The Secret Service also has its Uniform Division which protects the official foreign missions in the Washington area. This organiza- tion was formerly known as the Executive Protective Service or the White House Police. The scope of their responsi- bility was expanded to include these facilities in 1970 as the result of concern for street crime in the Washington area. In 1974, as a result of terrorist activity, a change in the statutory ceiling of manpower for the Uniform Division was received, authorizing an increase from 850 to 1200 men.[22]

Both pressures within and without government drove the Treasury department to seek this increase. The security of the diplomatic community within the United States was a concern not only to foreign governments but also the Department of State, which is sensitive to treaty obligations and reciprocity agreements with other countries. Treasury was of the opinion that a much more assertive policy of foreign diplomatic protection must be undertaken. This would involve not only an increased Uniform Division but also agreements with various cities (e.g., New York, Chicago, Los Angeles, Houston, Miami, San Francisco) to reimburse local police jurisdictions for the additional security provided the diplomatic missions. Local agencies were not always interested in supporting what in their view was a federal responsibility.

In October 1980 Secretary Edmund Muskie and Secretary G. William Miller sought approval from the Office of Management and Budget to increase Uniform Division personnel and support legislation, enabling State to reimburse local police for the security provided to diplomatic locations. Treasury was of the opinion that within the Washington area the U.S. Secret Service Uniform Division had served as a very effective deterrent to terrorist activity. However, its ability to fulfill its mission had been eroded because of the imposition of manpower reductions. Combined with increased requests for protection, this created the perception that Treasury was less than responsive to both State and embassy requests.[23] This concern is quite justified when it is noted that though there is a ceiling of 1200 officers established for the Uniform Division, only 800 positions are filled (in actuality). Within this number, approximately 350 have duties at the White House or the vice presidential residence. When administrative, training, and other functions are considered, only 330 officers are available to cover the 410 diplomatic sites in Washington, D.C. Treasury officials are of the opinion that without a substantial increase in personnel it cannot adequately fulfill its mission.[24] As America makes its demands upon other nations for protection of its personnel abroad, other nations may well demand a form of reciprocity that the U.S. cannot or will not provide. In December 1980, it became clear to the Treasury department that the request would not be granted. The OMB reply stated that the money for the extra 400 Uniform Division personnel should be handled through routine budgetary processes and the funding for municipalities would require more study. This issue was appealed and State has provided strong support for Treasury's efforts, but the matter became buried among the many problems of the new administration. This particular issue, the protection of diplomats in the Washington area, has been the one matter of most concern for the Treasury with the early Working Group and the current Executive Committee. Despite eight years of effort it has not yet been resolved.[25]

Another organizational interest concerning terrorism is due to the Treasury department's control of the U.S. Customs Service. As part of its function this agency interdicts and seizes contraband, processes persons, carries cargo and mail into and out of the U.S., and detects and apprehends persons engaged in fraudulent practices designed to circumvent customs laws. The role of the agency would be prevention of terrorism through the identification of a terrorist either entering or exiting the country. The Customs Service also worked closely with the FAA in providing security for U.S. air carriers (sky marshals) as described above.[26]

Within the department itself there has been no significant organizational change as a direct result of the terrorism problem. Rather, existing officers and bureaus have broadened their scope to meet the threat.[27]

Department of Justice

The interest of the Department of Justice stems from the fact that "acts constituting 'terrorism,' as we define it, are crimes. . . ."[28] The responsibility for overseeing the federal response to this phenomenon occurring within the United States rests with the Attorney General who had, in turn, delegated it to the Deputy Attorney General. The Deputy was to make "major policy decisions during a terrorism crisis."[29] While the president may choose to participate in the handling of an incident of great magnitude, it is assumed "that the response would be under the direction of the Department of Justice in, again, a domestic incident."[30] Under the Reagan administration these functions are now under the Associate Attorney General.

Within the department the lead agency for the management of a terrorist case would be the FBI. In a tactical sense, the special agent-in-charge at the scene would supervise under the control of the FBI director. The Deputy Attorney General was to be responsible for policy decisions and any legal judgements relating to the resolution of the case.

The FBI, since 1972, has prepared standard operating procedures and contingency plans for all fifty-nine field offices relating to terrorism and hijacking. Organizational modifications were made in the sense that special weapons and assault team (SWAT) capabilities were developed and hostage negotiators were trained and assigned to field offices.[31] Additionally, within the Criminal Investigations Division of FBI headquarters a Terrorism Section was created in April 1977. Beyond this, the actual organizational change has been minimal.[32]

The Department of Justice opposed the creation of an Assistant Attorney General for Terrorism Matters as suggested in the Omnibus Antiterrorism Act. This change was viewed as downgrading the responsibility in the department. Since the Deputy Attorney General already had "general oversight responsibilities of all elements of the Department that deal with matters of terrorism. . . . he is in a better position to coordinate, we think, than a separate and specialized office would be."[33]

Under the purview of the Deputy Attorney General was the Emergency Program Center which was concerned with civil disturbances, issues related to nuclear matters (peacetime -- i.e., disappearance of material, nuclear

extortion), and terrorism. The office was normally staffed
by four individuals to include the secretary. However,
during a crisis, the staff would be augmented as needed.
The Director served as deputy chairman of both the Executive Committee and the Working Group. Further, he was
chairman of the Contingency Planning and Crisis Management Committee (Domestic) and co-chairman of the Security
Policy Committee (Domestic). Terrorism, as in other agencies, was viewed as <u>one</u> issue versus <u>the</u> issue.[34]

It should be mentioned that during the policy staffing
prior to the issuance of PRM 30, a bureaucratic battle was
fought between State and Justice. The Department of Justice was concerned that if State chaired the Executive
Committee, too much emphasis would be given to the international arena. It was Justice's desire that there be a
co-chairmanship, that is both Justice and State, to help
insure adequate concentration on domestic terrorism. Representatives at State saw this as an attempt to wrest
control of the committee and actually assume chairmanship. Having interviewed representatives of both agencies, it appears that State, seeing Justice's efforts as
a significant threat, fought long and hard to maintain
control in their department. Justice, on the other hand,
was attempting to insure emphasis in lieu of taking control and accordingly conducted less of a battle. As has
been indicated, State maintained the chairmanship with
Justice as deputy. However, one Justice representative
felt that the position of deputy chairman was basically
meaningless and that the office was treated much more as
a committee member than as a deputy. There had been little
or no prior coordination or policy consultation that was
not equally discussed with all members of the Executive
Committee.[35]

It should be noted that representatives of one of
the other agencies that would soon be part of the Executive Committee initially supported State's desire to re-
tain chairmanship. This was not so much on the merits
of the issue but rather based upon the perception of the
then Deputy Attorney General as an "incompetent political
hack." The agency in the end supported Justice, allowing
that the incumbent would eventually be gone and it was
more proper for Justice to at least co-chair the committee.[36]

One agency within the Department that had a good
deal of concern with the nation's preparedness to combat
terrorism is the Law Enforcement Assistance Administration
(LEAA). The Administration was not an operational agency,
but one whose "mandate with respect to terrorism is
primarily limited to the support of research and training
activities."[37] LEAA's concern with terrorism stemmed
mainly from the 1973 Amendments to the Omnibus Crime
Control and Safe Streets Act of 1968. Additionally, LEAA

had authority to provide support to state and local law
enforcement agencies on all domestic criminal justice
matters, including terrorism. Through its association
with the Working Group, LEAA attempted to promote
problem-oriented projects and avoid duplication of efforts by other federal agencies. "Our experience has
been that the Working Group has proved invaluable as a
vehicle for the exchange of information and the coordination of national counterterrorism research strategy."[38]
While LEAA was authorized to make grants independently,
"the major portion of our funding for research on international terrorism has been through the Working Group."[39]
Between 1973 and the latter part of 1978, thirty-six projects were initiated in this regard, directly obligating
$5,540,294 for projects directly bearing on terrorism
and skyjacking. Of that total: $1,225,446 went for
international and domestic research; $2,061,452 toward
airport security research and training; and $2,163,396
toward the training of state and local law enforcement
personnel. The scope of these research projects was
pervasive throughout all levels of government and, as
such, LEAA's influence had been significant.

It is alleged that because of an LEAA sponsored
study, PRM 30 evolved. Robert H. Kupperman, Phd., Chief
Scientist of the Arms Control and Disarmament Agency,
undertook a study in 1974-75 funded by LEAA relative to
crises management in terrorist situations. The study indicated that the U.S. government was weak in this regard
and adequate structure to fully function during a large
scale terrorist attack was lacking. The study was made
available through the old Working Group to the NSC. When
the Carter administration came into office, it was recognized that the issue should be addressed.[40]

It should be mentioned that LEAA today is fighting
for its organizational life and the prognosis is guarded.
The events leading to its demise illustrate some of the
classic dilemmas confronted by organizations. Originally
created as the Office of Law Enforcement Assistance in
1965 it was part of a nationally directed effort to discover the causes of crime and better train police officers.
By 1968 the Office had sanctioned 330 projects at a cost
of nineteen million dollars. Throughout 1967 and 1968
the nation's mood began to change and instead of attempting to attack the root causes of crime (poverty, unemploy-
ment, etc.) more concern was focused on upgrading police
effectiveness. The Office of Law Enforcement Assistance
became the Law Enforcement Assistance Administration (LEAA).
In 1969 alone, LEAA was authorized one hundred million
dollars for activities relating to law enforcement planning,
training, education, and research.[41] In 1973 the goal of
the nation's anti-crime effort was modified again and LEAA
was to concern itself with improving all facets of the

criminal justice system to include not only police but
the courts, corrections, and juvenile problems.[42] By 1976
LEAA had provided state and local governments more than
four billion dollars in support of 80,000 criminal justice
programs but there were no signs that crime in the U.S.
had abated.[43] In 1979 President Carter signed a bill
in another attempt to better organize the nation's effort
to combat crime. LEAA became a division under a newly
created Office of Justice Assistance, Research and
Statistics (OJARS), whose purpose was to coordinate and
support not only LEAA but also three other agencies.[44]

On paper it appeared feasible, in reality it has
been described as sheer anarchy, with many blurred
lines of authority. With the bureaus under OJARS headed
by a presidential appointee, each tended to act independently as if OJARS did not exist.[45] Additionally, the
eleven year history of LEAA saw ten different administrators
and numerous redefinitions of goals. Such institutionalized confusion would be very hard to correct with a mere
realignment of agencies. LEAA itself had its funds cut
away from under it in what was described as the budget
balancing "March massacre" by President Carter.

The Immigration and Naturalization Service, which
has been in existence since 1891, is concerned with terrorism through its responsibility to control the admis-
sion, exclusion, and deportation of aliens. Additionally,
it is responsible for guarding against the illegal entry
of persons into the United States. Through the use of
its enforcement arms, to include the Border Patrol, INS
would seek to identify and neutralize terrorists before
they could carry out their acts. The Immigration and
Nationality Act of June 27, 1952, as amended, is very
specific concerning who may enter this country and who
may be subsequently deported. Prior conduct as well as
intended conduct believed to be counter to the interests
of the United States could be enough to deny entry or
cause deportation.[46] Specific modification of the Act,
therefore, to include terrorism is not deemed necessary.

Department of Defense

A good deal has already been said about DOD involvement in domestic counterterrorist activity in Chapter 5.
It was indicated then that, in addition to organizational
considerations, significant sociological and legal aspects
would play heavily in decisions to employ military force.
The use of armed forces would be considered only when
control of the situation is clearly beyond the capability
of local, state, and federal enforcement authorities. The
president would decide, based upon the advice of the
attorney general, and it would be a "last resort in extreme
cases of highly sophisticated or large-scale para-military

terrorist operations."[47] Once the decision was made, the
president or his designee (the attorney general or his
representative) would establish a specific military objective and the degree of force authorized. Within the
assigned mission, the military unit would function under
the tactical command of the military commander. The
overall control of the federal response would be retained
by civil authorities.[48]

In a situation of lesser magnitude (i.e., a terrorist hijacking of a military aircraft) DOD, under the provisions of the Air Transportation Security Act of 1974,
must defer to the FAA. It would be up to an FAA official
to decide, "after considering fully the expressed wishes
of the pilot-in-command and the DOD designated official,
whether law enforcement action is appropriate."[49] If
law enforcement is deemed appropriate, the FAA official
is to request the FBI to take the needed action. It is
interesting to note that the memorandum was signed four
years after the Act was passed.

It has been suggested that DOD did not significantly
become actively involved in the government's counterterror
effort until 1978. There are several reasons, from an
organizational perspective, for this. Primarily, there
was the perception concerning the traditional role of DOD
elements in any law enforcement activity within the United
States. Coupled with this is the fact that terrorism, as
opposed to issues such as strategic arms limitations, mutual force reductions in Europe, or acquisition of major
weapon systems, was not a problem central to DOD. As a
result, it was often placed on the back burner. It was
the result of PRM 30 and the subsequent reorganization
of the government's structure to combat terrorism that
gave the issue the predominance needed to be considered
more extensively. Since then DOD (as well as other government departments) has cooperated to a far greater
degree.[50]

While some have alleged that terrorism was viewed
as a back burner issue, others within DOD have a slightly differing perspective. Terrorism, unlike matters such
as arms control and mutual balanced force reductions, is
a matter for which policy can be determined once and for
all. This being done, the issue for the policy makers
ceases to demand their attention. Thereafter, once policy
has been established, other actors in DOD (i.e., the Joint
Chiefs of Staff or the separate services) may become very
much involved in building forces and insuring capability.
Thus, the importance of the issue does not decrease, rather the locus of emphasis may move from the office of
the secretary to the Joint Chiefs of Staff or elsewhere.[51]

On January 9, 1978, Secretary of Defense Harold Brown
directed that a Counter-Terrorism Steering Committee be
formed, chaired by the assistant secretary of defense for

International Security Affairs. Permanent membership
was to include the director or a senior representative
of the Joint Staff and the director, Defense Intelligence
Agency, or a senior representative. Other personnel would
be invited by the chairman as the circumstances warranted.
The committee, in its consideration of the terrorist
threat, was to ensure that problem areas would be identified and addressed at the policy level and ensure that
DOD interests are adequately represented in the interagency arena. [52] The committee was actively used since
its inception to bring relevant issues to the fore. Since
other personnel could be invited as deemed necessary by
the chairman, the committee was effective in bringing
forth views that might have been otherwise buried as
they floated up through levels of the hierarchy.[53] However, it should be noted that the committee had nothing
to do with the planning of the Iranian mission and has
not been active in the early Reagan administration.

In May 1979, Senator Ribicoff wrote to Secretary
Brown expressing concern over DOD's counterterrorist
forces. Based upon testimony of representatives of the
Airline Pilots Association, Ribicoff had been led to
believe that the military forces "have virtually no detailed training for rescuing hostages from hijacked aircraft . . . . I believe the Department of Defense should
work closely with these groups (pilots and the airline
industry) in developing highly specialized counter-terrorist units."[54] Senator Ribicoff was informed that training
for such contingencies had, in fact, been conducted with
the FAA and FBI.

> With the cooperation of the Federal Aviation
> Administration and several major airlines, DOD
> counter-terrorist forces have trained on all
> types of commercial airliners for situations
> requiring rescue of hostages. These forces
> have also trained at several major airports
> to ensure they are thoroughly knowledgeable
> of airport operations. The training has been
> conducted discretely to prevent disclosure
> of techniques, tactics, and personnel that would
> be used during an actual incident. As a result,
> the Air Line Pilots Association was most prob-
> ably unaware that such training had been con-
> ducted.[55]

It is the concern for secrecy of tactics and capabilities which limits an extensive examination of the organizational aspects of DOD's counterterror efforts.

Prior to his taking over as Secretary of Defense,
Caspar W. Weinberger recognized this dilemma. In testimony before Congress he said, "that describing the

country's anti-terrorist capabilities might compromise
a future operation, but that keeping them secret was
preventing him from sending a strong message to potential terrorists."[56]

What is discernable is that in the wake of the Iran
failure, the Joint Chiefs of Staff established a counterterrorist task force that is secret in name, numbers of
personnel, and location. The unit is alleged to be composed of representatives of all services and concerning
itself with tactics, intelligence and operational planning. Whether it would direct a counterterrorist mission,
partake in one, or both is kept a tightly held secret.[57]

Central Intelligence Agency

No information other than what has been reported
in Chapter 4 relating the CIA's response to terrorism
can be provided. Agency concern for covert sources and
techniques precluded an examination of that organization.

Department of Energy

The agency was established by the Department of
Energy Organization Act of 1977. The Act consolidated
the major federal energy functions into one cabinet-level
department. The responsibilities of the Energy Research
and Development Administration, the Federal Power Commission, the Federal Energy Administration, several regional
offices, as well as functions of the Interstate Commerce
Commission and the departments of Commerce, Housing and
Urban Development, the Navy, and the Interior were included.[58] The primary concern of DOE in the counterterrorist
area is the adequate safeguarding of special nuclear materials and nuclear facilities from theft and sabotage.
Special nuclear materials (SNM) are plutonium, uranium-
233, and enriched uranium (U-235). These are the materials that could potentially be used in attempts to make
nuclear explosives or in an extortion scheme. Within the
U.S. the actual safeguarding is carried out by contract
operators working within policies established by DOE.
Should the active deterrents (guards, protection alarms,
target hardening, etc.) fail, DOE has developed operating
procedures to minimize threats to the public.[59] Should
there be a determination that a criminal violation has
taken place, it would be the responsibility of the FBI
to investigate.

While the DOE is a recent creation, the safeguard
function was previously under the purview of the Energy
Research and Development Administration which was part
of the Working Group assisting the original Cabinet Committee to Combat Terrorism. ERDA was very much aware

of the potential threat posed by terrorists and recognized it "as a factor requiring explicit attention."[60] The administration began a comprehensive analysis to identify motivations and capabilities of terrorist groups who could pose a threat to nuclear plants and SNM. This policy was continued under the Department of Energy.[61]

The need for strict safeguards was clearly apparent from data compiled by ERDA and submitted to Senator Ribicoff's committee during the 1978 hearings. A total of ninety-one incidents involving threats of violence or actual acts were noted between 1969 and 1977. Most were bomb threats; some involved pipe bombs found near facilities and the apparent breaching of the outer security areas. During this same period the Nuclear Regulatory Commission reported 194 similar incidents against commercial facilities.[62]

In February 1979, DOE published Order 5632.2 relating to the protection of special nuclear materials. The order complemented other standard operating procedures in efforts to deter, prevent and counteract "the theft of SNM by an adversary with or without inside collaboration."[63] The order is designed to bring about the implementation of procedures for facilities throughout the nation by establishing minimum standards applicable to all. It was further designed to provide comparable effectiveness with that required of licensees by the Nuclear Regulatory Commission.[64]

It is apparent that, even though significant organizational change has taken place among the government agencies responsible for our energy programs, there remained a continual concern for security and the threat of terrorist activity. The names of particular offices may have been changed, but the mission was not. Other representatives on the Executive Committee have commented quite favorably concerning the efforts of DOE in this regard. While it may be single issue involvement it has been quite extensive, making use of inhouse and outside (Rand, Sandia Lab) capabilities to identify weaknesses and rectify them.

National Security Council

Information relating to the NSC has been set forth in Chapter 4. As a result of PRM 30 (which is classified), the federal government's response to terrorism was reorganized under the aegis of the Special Coordination Committee whose chairman was always the assistant to the president for national security affairs. It was expected that the SCC would directly exercise its responsibilities only in the event of a major terrorist incident requiring the highest level decisions. In all other cases the incident would be managed by the lead agency.

Additionally, should interagency disputes arise concerning terrorism, the NSC would act to resolve the issue. Zbigniew Brzezinski instructed that both the ECT and its Working Group's primary concern would be policy coordination and information exchange and not the management of specific terrorist incidents. This was to be the responsibility of the lead agency or, in large cases, the NSC itself. In interviews with officials closely related to the government's counterterrorist efforts, two individuals described the NSC at that time as being of two minds concerning terrorism. On one hand, it was a terrible problem that could not be tolerated and harsh countermeasures were to be implemented. Conversely, if a large terrorist crisis developed and there was a real danger of death and destruction, the NSC would "almost go to war to keep the issue from getting near to them."[65]

It is interesting to note the relationship over the years between the NSC and the apparatus established to deal with terrorism. In the early period a senior advisor to the NSC attended meetings of the original Working Group. The Cabinet Committee, having met only once, allowed the Working Group to deal with the important issues. This was quite significant, for the Working Group functioned operationally and actually formulated policy.[66] The NSC representative saw himself as one participant among several and also as "the president's ear."[67] President Nixon at that time was very much concerned with terrorist happenings. After each meeting of the Working Group the NSC advisor would prepare a memo so that Henry Kissinger would be able to keep the president abreast of activities. There existed a genuine concern both within the White House and among those on the Working Group that the terrorism problem was quite serious and had to be dealt with quickly.[68] This, coupled with clear instructions to all agencies to cooperate in the counterterror effort, helped assure productive output. When significant issues needed resolution it was not a matter for the NSC representative to return and present options to Henry Kissinger for review. Rather, Armin Meyer would consult with Secretary Rogers and then prepare a correspondence for his signature which would go to the White House. To the best of his knowledge the NSC advisor during the 1972-73 period could not recall even having to ask the NSC for permission so that the Working Group could undertake a particular task.[69]

Another member of the Working Group who was present during the 1973-74 period confirmed the general lack of bureaucratic battling at the time. Issues and policy were hammered out among members of the Group and, while differences in opinion were evident, the overriding concern tended to remain attempting to come to grips with the problem. As time went on through 1974 and 1975 the

Working Group tended to meet less and less. While Ambassador Meyer was chief coordinator the group met at
least weekly. During Hoffacker's tenure it met once every
two weeks and may have even slipped to once a month when
Fearey headed the Working Group.[70]

One individual who has served both as a member of
the original Working Group and the Executive Committee
views the decision making process in a slightly different
light. He cannot recall presenting a series of options
which were sent forward to the NSC. If the matter
affected the Department of State it was treated in much
more detail and Meyer and or Secretary Rogers may well
have presented the issue to the NSC or the president.
This was more a matter of self-interest (State) than the
concern of the Working Group itself. The Working Group
did prepare some summaries of their activities which did
go to the White House but this should not be confused
with the raising of issues.[71]

This description of the Working Group's activity
should not be viewed as State being concerned only with
itself. While the element of self-interest was obvious,
many of the issues being confronted (i.e., U.N. action,
bilateral and multilateral agreements, protection of facilities abroad) were of great interest to the department.

Concerning the matter of White House or NSC leadership, it was noted that other than President Nixon's
public statements on terrorism (see Chapter 6) there was
virtually no policy direction to the Working Group.[72]

The relationship of the NSC to the Executive Committee was quite different. (I will not examine the Working
Group since it changed considerably over the years. It
bears little resemblance to its predecessor and has been
described by some Executive Committee members as more fa-
cade than substance, and worthy of little attention.)
The initiation of PRM 30 by the president through the
NSC gave rise to a governmental review of the U. S.
policy towards terrorism. The study group was composed
of representatives from the agencies that currently make
up the interagency group. Issues were raised, assigned
to sub-committees, staffed, and policy proposals formulated. Issues that were irreconcilable were not presented to the NSC for resolution.[73] Rather, during a
final session, David Aron, a member of Brzezinski's
staff, made the final decisions on all the outstanding
matters. This was done in a rather matter of fact way
(one described it as high handed), where issue after
issue was raised and settled as Aron deemed fit.[74]

While a great deal of data had been staffed and
presented by the various committees they were not incor-
porated as part of PRM 30. Due to a concern for leaks
to the press, hundreds of pages were reduced to two.
While the content of the document is classified it

basically states that terrorism was a problem that must be dealt with and established the Executive Committee and Working Group to do just that. The document is more significant for what it does not say. It did not give the chairman of the Executive Committee authority to ensure other agencies' cooperation. The status quo was institutionalized, i.e., the Department of Justice would concern itself with domestic terrorism and the Department of State would look to external threats.[75] One observer commented that the NSC found itself facing an issue that it really did not feel was too important, but which was perceived by many to be a problem. When you seek to solve a nonissue within government one does what is most logical (bureaucratically speaking) and create a committee.[76] The NSC never had in mind that the Executive Committee would be more than a forum for coordination. True to its mandate, the Executive Committee did not assign policy papers to its member agencies, formulate any decisional issues nor present option papers to the NSC for final decisions. The minutes of the meetings tended to resemble items on an agenda and rarely, if ever, did they show any discord by the committee membership. It could be said that the authority given the Executive Committee during the Carter administration was directly proportional to the NSC perception of the threat of terrorism.[77]

NOTES

1. "Cabinet Committee Redoubles its Efforts to Combat Terrorism," Department of State Newsletter, April 1973, p. 12.
2. Interview with John N. Gatch, January 24, 1980. Gatch had served in Kuwait and Bahrain.
3. "Heck Leads New Effort to Combat Terrorism," Department of State Newsletter, August-September 1976, p. 13.
4. "Statement by President Nixon," Department of State Bulletin, October 23, 1972, p. 476.
5. Testimony of Robert Fearey, U.S. Congress, Senate, Committee on the Judiciary, Terroristic Activity, International Terrorism, Hearings, 1st session, May 14, 1975, p. 214.
6. Interviews with individuals either currently or previously assigned to the Office to Combat Terrorism, January 24, 1980.
7. Ibid. Additional interviews with personnel with a working knowledge of the Office to Combat Terrorism, January 21-28, 1980. Nine interviews were conducted.
8. Interview with staff personnel, House of Representatives, Committee on the Judiciary, February 29, 1980.

9. Interviews with members of the Security Policy Committee and Crisis Management Committees, January 25 and 27, February 27, June 10 and 12, 1980.

10. The Washington Post, January 29, 1981, p. 1.

11. Testimony of Richard T. Kennedy before the Senate Foreign Relations Committee, June 10, 1981, Current Policy # 285, U.S. Department of State, Bureau of Public Affairs, Washington, D.C.

12. Brian M. Jenkins and Janera Johnson, International Terrorism: A Chronology 1968-1974 (Santa Monica, CA: The RAND Corporation, R-1597-DOS/ARPA, 1975), pp. 24-25.

13. U.S. News and World Report, September 21, 1970, p. 17.

14. Interview with FAA officials with a close and continuing relationship with aviation security, January 28, 1980.

15. Interview with Federal Aviation Administration official, Department of Transportation, January 17, 1980.

16. Ibid., February 12, 1980.

17. Ibid., June 6, 1980.

18. United States Government Manual 1979-1980 (Washington: U.S. Govt. Print. Off., May 1979), p. 440.

19. Memorandum of Understanding Between the Director, Federal Bureau of Investigation and Commandant, United States Coast Guard Concerning a Policy of Mutual Assistance in Support of Coast Guard/Federal Bureau of Investigation Operations to Counteract Terrorist Activity in a Maritime Environment, signed by William H. Webster, Director, FBI, March 23, 1979, and John B. Hayes, Commandant, USCG, on April 17, 1979. The briefness of the MOU leaves a great deal open for interpretation by each agency.

20. Interview with Commander A. Robert Matt, Intelligence and Security Division, U.S. Coast Guard, June 11, 1980.

21. Ibid.

22. Interview with Treasury Department official with a working knowledge of that agency's role in combating terrorism, June 9, 1980. An article in The New York Times, June 10, 1980, p. 10, indicated that there were 812 officers in the Uniform Division. The article quoted William P. DeCourcy of the State Department's Office of Security as saying the creation of the Uniform Division "can be traced back to the upsurge of terrorism around the world." Washington, D.C., is the only location for the Uniform Division. In 1975 President Ford vetoed a bill that would have expanded the force to guard diplomatic missions outside Washington. This remains the responsibility of local agencies.

23. Interview with Robert McBrien, Office of the Assistant Secretary for Enforcement and Operations, U.S. Department of

the Treasury, November 17, 1980.

24. Ibid.

25. Ibid., December 18, 1980.

26. Interviews with Treasury and FAA officials, January 28, June 9, 1980.

27. Interview with Treasury Department officials, February 27 and June 9, 1980.

28. Testimony of Benjamin Civiletti, Deputy Attorney General, U.S. Congress, House Committee on the Judiciary, Federal Capabilities in Crisis Management and Terrorism, Hearings (95th Congress, 2nd session, 1978), p. 14.

29. Ibid., p. 4.

30. Ibid.

31. Testimony of Sebastian S. Mignosa, Terrorism Section Chief, FBI, U.S. Congress, Senate, Committee on Governmental Affairs, An Act to Combat International Terrorism, Hearings (S. 2236, 1978), p. 212.

32. Interview with FBI official closely associated with their counterterrorist effort, January 28, 1980.

33. Testimony of Mary G. Lawton, Deputy Assistant Attorney General, An Act to Combat International Terrorism, p. 209.

34. Interview with Department of Justice official familiar with that agency's antiterrorist capability, January 28, 1980.

35. Interviews with members of the Executive Committee to Combat Terrorism, January 21, 28 and December 4, 1980.

36. Interview with member of the Executive Committee to Combat Terrorism, December 18, 1980.

37. Testimony of Perry Rivkind, Assistant Administrator, LEAA, Federal Capabilities in Crisis Management, p. 83.

38. Ibid., p. 83.

39. Ibid.

40. Interview with former LEAA official who was intimately concerned with that agency's counterterror efforts during the 1970's, December 16, 1980.

41. Joseph Bunce, "Crime in the Streets: A National Policy Issue," unpublished paper, undated, p. 7.

42. Ibid., p. 11.

43. Ibid., p. 15.

44. Ibid., p. 18.

45. Interview with former LEAA official, December 19, 1980.

46. For excerpts of the Act, see Center for Policy Research, National Governors' Association, Domestic Terrorism (Washington: U.S. Govt. Print. Off., May 1979), p. D-1 through D-10.

47. Testimony of Ambassador Anthony Quainton, U.S. Congress, House, Committee on the Judiciary, Federal Capabilities in Crisis Management and Terrorism, p. 49.

48. Ibid.

49. Memorandum of Understanding Between the Department of Transportation and the Department of Defense Concerning Aircraft Piracy, signed by C. W. Duncan, Jr., Deputy Secretary of Defense, August 7, 1978, and Alan Butchman, Deputy Secretary of Transportation, September 7, 1978, p. 4.

50. Interviews with civilian and military representatives associated with DOD's counterterrorist program, January 23, February 25, and February 28, 1980.

51. Interview with Franklin D. Kramer, Assistant Secretary of Defense for International Security Affairs, December 2, 1980.

52. Memorandum concerning the "Establishment of a DOD Counter-Terrorism Steering Committee," from the Secretary of Defense, dated January 9, 1978.

53. Interview with Franklin D. Kramer, December 2, 1980.

54. Letter from Senator Abe Ribicoff to Harold Brown, May 7, 1979.

55. Letter from John L. Naler (Department of the Army) to Senator Ribicoff, June 12, 1979. Discussion by the writer with FAA officials substantiated these comments.

56. The New York Times, February 3, 1981, p. B-13.

57. Ibid.

58. U.S. Government Manual, p. 251.

59. Department of Energy, Fact Sheet, "DOE Safeguards on Nuclear Materials, Facilities" (Washington: Office of Public Affairs, July 1978), p. 2.

60. ERDA Fact Sheet, "Safeguards" (Washington: ERDA, October 1978), p. 5.

61. See Peter deLeon, Brian Jenkins, Konrad Kellen, Joseph Krofcheck, Attributes of Potential Criminal Adversaries of U.S. Nuclear Programs (Santa Monica, CA: The RAND Corporation, R-2225-SL, February 1978).

62. An Act to Combat Terrorism, pp. 71, 640-644.

63. U.S. Department of Energy, Order 5632.2, February 16, 1979, p. 1.

64. Ibid., p. 2.

65. Interviews with U.S. government personnel intimately involved with the counterterrorist effort, January and February, 1980.

66. Interview with Thompson Crockett, former Department of Justice representative on the Executive Committee to Combat Terrorism, December 4, 1980.

67. Interview with Osborn Day, former senior advisor to the NSC and member of the original Working Group, December 4, 1980.

68. Ibid. Day advised that his comments were from memory and should be weighed with that in mind.

69. Ibid.

70. Interview with John N. Gatch, December 9, 1980.

71. Interview with a member who had served on the original Working Group and Executive Committee, December 19, 1980.

72. Ibid.

73. Interview with Thompson Crockett, December 4, 1980.

74. Interview with two former members of the Executive Committee on Terrorism, December 4, 1980 and January 13, 1981.

75. Interview with Thompson Crockett, December 4, 1980.

76. Interview with a member of the Executive Committee to Combat Terrorism, December 5, 1980.

77. Interview with Thompson Crockett, December 4, 1980.

8
Conclusions

It has often been said that terrorism is a growth industry. This is not only based upon the increasing number of incidents during the 1970s, but also because a good deal more writer's ink than victim's blood may have been spilled dealing with the problem.

Terrorism is directed at the institutions or personages holding social and/or political power. Within a democracy the methods of countering the phenomenon are rather limited. The government, in the defense of certain values, must employ techniques which will preserve them. Overreaction, general suppression of rights, censorship and the use of a secret police could all backfire in an alienation of the populace. Yet, the careful and judicious handling of a terrorist situation is a very difficult task demanding timely and effective actions by the various government agencies concerned.

It was pointed out in the first part of this study that industrialized nations such as the United States are quite vulnerable to terrorist attacks. Interdependent automated systems, commercial aircraft, natural gas or oil pipelines, electrical power grids and off-shore oil rigs are all examples of sabotage-prone targets whose destruction would have significant impact. New York City in the late 1970s sustained a serious power outage when lightning completely disrupted the Consolidated Edison system. With ten million people immobilized, the blackout gave rise to a climate that saw thousands of looters take to the streets resulting in 3,300 arrests, over 100 policemen injured and damage costing approximately $150 million dollars. The major point to be learned is that if an "act of nature" produced a two-day siege, a dedicated trained terrorist group could easily produce an equal or greater crisis should they so choose.

What makes the United States a prime target for a terrorist attack is the heavy attention the media will provide the event. This immediate and extensive coverage by television, radio, and the press would enable

terrorists to gain extensive publicity. While to date
no personage of high political office has been taken hostage by terrorists in the United States, the notoriety
surrounding Patty Hearst's abduction is a ready reminder
of the making of a media event.

Any terrorist crisis would be newsworthy and the
attending publicity could well be the deciding factor
determining the need for presidential involvement. Further, there could well be interplay among the media, the
victim, the terrorists, and enforcement personnel. No
clear lines exist to delineate the right of news people
to cover an event and the officials' responsibility to
resolve the matter. The police or federal officers may
find themselves on duty for prolonged periods, having
their own difficulties in command and control. City managers, politicians, or others in government may be on the
scene seeking information and/or issuing statements. The
demands for data originate, therefore, from several sources,
and could easily be viewed as distracting by enforcement
personnel. Additionally, there is a valid concern that
representatives of the media may usurp the role of the
negotiator in the crisis. Short of this, media contact
with the terrorists may enhance their (the terrorists)
sense of power by insuring public awareness of their
strength and cause. Additionally, there is the long-
standing fear that all the notoriety may well serve as
an inspiration for others to carry out similar acts.

The media perspective centers on the right of the
public to be informed. In addition, the media are highly competitive with a powerful, commercial incentive that
drives much, if not all, of their activity. Responsible
reporters seek accurate information and take issue with
those who interfere with this goal. Ideally, the media
should seek to report all and only the facts, striking a
balance between the action of the terrorists and the official response. But as indicated in this study, terrorism is theater, and the intensity of the event blurs
the judgment of those seeking to balance the right to
know, with the duty to report while considering safety
of the hostages. The very reporting of the act can
change the character of the event itself. The use of
vocabulary, tone of voice, and pictures broadcast from
the scene, all have the potential for forming public opinion as the event unfolds. If a terrorist incident were
to take place in an area of high population density, in-
flammatory reporting could well lead to general public
disorder.

Perhaps the greatest difficulty in coming to grips
with terrorism is the problem of determining its nature
and scope. Data presented in Chapter 6 indicated that
the threat posed by terrorists is not a constant, it
waxes and wanes. The number of groups and the frequency

and location of events have varied over the years. Some
groups have shown themselves capable of carrying out very
sophisticated campaigns involving kidnapping, the use
of safe houses, and underground networks, along with complex communication methods. Other groups have all they
can do to successfully detonate a bomb at a targeted site,
rather than on their lap. Additionally, as shown in
Chapter 2, terrorism may be committed for several purposes:
wringing specific concessions, gaining publicity, creating
widespread disorder, provoking repression, coercing cooperation and obedience, or as an attempt to punish. Accordingly, the organizations that must deal with terrorism
view the problem from various perspectives. It can be a
criminal matter, a political matter, or an issue centering
on maritime or aviation security -- to mention just a
few. This perceptual diversity compounds the problem of
developing a unified response.

Organizations such as the United Nations have yet to
arrive at an acceptable definition of terrorism. Despite
this, international conventions have been drawn up dealing with aspects of terrorism, i.e., kidnapping and hijacking. While arguments concerning who is a terrorist
and who is a freedom fighter go on, these particular manifestations of terrorism have been addressed. It should
be noted that the terms freedom fighter and terrorist
are not mutually exclusive. Freedom fighter can be
used in relation to the ultimate end or goal (e.g.,
emancipation, liberation) of a particular group. The
means employed in pursuit of that goal may well be
terrorist in nature.

This study proffered a definition where terrorism
was seen as a purposeful human political activity, primarily directed toward the creation of a general climate
of fear and designed to influence, in ways desired by the
protagonist, other human beings and, through them, some
course of events. It was also noted that there is a
fine line between government sponsored terror and terrorism undertaken by groups. Government acts often
appear as law enforcement and formally adhere or give the
impression of adhering, to the law. Where the legislation
is lacking, government terror is made to appear justified
through such actions as a declaration of a state of emergency and the issuing of decrees. Terrorist groups, on
the other hand, make little or no pretense at legality
and often engage in open defiance of the law.

As far as can be determined for the United States,
within a particular government agency the issue of terrorism may not be viewed as relevant to the central role
and mission. The Department of State, it will be recalled, saw the problem as one mainly occurring in the Middle
East. It was not until 1976 that the actual Office for
Combating Terrorism was established and it was not seen

as one of the main missions of State. Within the Department of Transportation, terrorism was viewed as one aspect of larger issues, aviation safety and maritime law enforcement. For the Department of the Treasury, terrorism was not viewed from a monetary or economic perspective, but rather from its lesser law enforcement role. For the Department of Defense -- where there is great concern for strategic forces, rapid deployment, NATO coordination, sea power projection, and the severe problems of adequate manpower -- it is understandable that interest is somewhat lacking in a small counterterrorist force that may never, or rarely, be used.

When addressing the military capability to combat terrorism, aspects of civil-military relations also should be addressed. As was pointed out earlier in the study, there are significant legal, political, and sociological factors that must be dealt with prior to the employment of military force. Clearly the need to call upon the military should not be considered unless regular law enforcement personnel are unable to handle the matter. Since civil authority has the primary purpose of maintaining law and order, and since this has remained a tradition throughout our nation's history, the bringing in of the military is a major policy decision. If such a decision is made it will go far beyond the basic employment of force. It will need to take into account how much force, under whose authority, utilization up to what point, and the possible affect upon public opinion. Of the many purposes for which terrorists conduct their activity, there are two which either attempt to have a government overreact or, by not reacting, show inherent weakness. Those who decide to make use of soldiers in lieu of police must heavily weigh these factors. Are they doing what is needed, or what the terrorists want?

If it is determined that the military is the solution, depending on the locus of the incident, true capability may be many hours away. Counterterrorist capabilities are rather limited commodities. Local and state civil authorities in any planning for terrorist activity should query nearby military units to determine what level of expertise is available should the need arise. Common knowledge of each other's capabilities is the first step in identifying weaknesses. At the national level various scenarios should be developed and studied. This would provide for the forethought relative to various legal hurdles should the president need to issue a proclamation bringing in federal troops. In a time-sensitive crisis, there will be little time for judicial debate.

This study has shown that as organizations identify a problem or situation which may have an impact on them, information and some element of control are sought. The development of the Working Group during the period 1972-

1979 is an example of this phenomena. From an original
membership of ten agencies, it evolved into a cluster of
more than thirty. This resulted in a restructuring along
functional lines to bring about more effective coordination. Yet, as indicated in Chapter 6, it appears that
some of the committee chairmen found it easier to deal
with members on a one-to-one basis rather than as part
of a fully constituted committee.

The chair agency for both the old Executive Committee
and the Working Group, as well as the new Interdepartmental Group, has remained the Department of State.
Initially (1972) this was based upon the perception that
terrorism was fundamentally a problem whose origin was
in the Middle East. Domestically, the Department of
Justice was to be the lead agency. What developed is
a policy coordination function for both internal and
external terrorism chaired by an ambassador and one or
more State Department personnel. The Department of Justice
remained as vice chairman (not co-chairman) throughout
the Carter administration. There was occasional friction
between the two departments as to the propriety of the
arrangement, yet State retained its chairmanship. Having
vested State with its role, it would be difficult to
diminish its authority. With Justice as the lead agency,
it, in fact, possessed all the functional power it needed
without the addition of a title such as chairman or co-
chairman.

Coupled with the interorganizational frictions which
hinder policy development, the weighting of the office
within the Department of State added to the problem. The
rotation of personnel and the location of the office within the department's hierarchy gave rise to the impression
that it was more a second cousin than a prime mover. As
the result of a presidential reorganization program in
1977, the Office for Combatting Terrorism was given the
additional sway needed to function more effectively.
This reorganization was viewed favorably by the other
agencies responsible for coordinating the efforts of their
own organizations. Additionally, in 1979, the position of
director of the Office to Combat Terrorism was awarded
the rank of ambassador and placed under the purview of
the deputy secretary. Previously, the title of ambassador
was the result of the director's former duties. Through
the early period of the Reagan administration the department is again attempting internal reorganization to enhance
its ability to counter terrorism. The prognosis is guarded,
for despite the increased rhetoric by the Secretary of
State, substantive change has not come about.

Considering all the interorganization difficulties,
the Executive Committee, as it was constituted, did serve
as an orderly means of interagency coordination. It was
small, having only seven agencies along with a repre-

sentative of the National Security Council. A degree of familiarity and trust developed, making frank discussions and recommendations possible. Those in attendance were of sufficient rank within their respective organizations to speak with authority concerning proposed policies and the degree to which their agencies would accept or reject them. In this regard it may be said that the interagency effort did evolve into a true coordination vehicle. The new Interdepartmental Group has had some initial difficulties in developing a similar cohesion. There has been some concern that State may be trying to exert itself too much, thereby causing friction to develop and lessening the willingness for all agencies to cooperate.

Another dilemma also remains. In any large-scale terrorist incident at home or abroad, will the organizations and structures in place be the ones employed? Will the natural tendency of the president to turn to those in whom he has the greatest confidence (regardless of the position held) cause him to overlook the programming and planning of those organizationally responsible for countering terrorism? From the evidence available concerning the Iran mission, the Department of State, the agency with operational responsibility for international incidents, disagreed with the view that a rescue mission was appropriate. Within the department, the Office for Combatting Terrorism was not a participant in the decision process--apparently only the secretary and the deputy secretary were involved. When the final determination was made, the Secretary of State was absent. He subsequently resigned in protest.

One of the privileges (or burdens) of the office of the president is that the incumbent can become involved in any issue he desires. He greatly influences the decision making process by setting the stage and determining who will play what role. A crisis allows the president a rare opportunity to truly lead. He can implement or ignore the organizational routines established to facilitate policy implementation. Even if the president wishes to keep his distance and allow established procedures to be followed, he may be drawn into the fray by forces beyond his control. The circumstances of the event, such as wide scale public disorder, may demand presidential involvement. Direct and instantaneous communications between nations could well result in the head of a foreign government telephoning the president demanding certain actions if representatives of his people are involved either as victims or perpetrators. The media could also escalate the event to the door of the White House. Within hours of the Iran mission, the mother of one of the hostages visiting Teheran, the Iranian foreign minister, the Soviet foreign minister, and the president all addressed a global audience via satellite. The office of the president then must be viewed as a key variable in any analysis of the response to terrorism.

The locus of the event, domestic or foreign, will also influence the nature of the response. There is a greater element of control when the act occurs within one's borders. The organizational actors involved are more finite than if the incident takes place on foreign soil. The Japanese experience is an excellent example in this regard. The most noteworthy acts of the Japanese Red Army happened outside their homeland. Domestically, the Japanese police, after some initial difficulty, were able to force the Red Army underground. When they undertook terrorist acts in Europe, Asia, and the Middle East, the Japanese government was quick to capitulate and pay ransom. The constraints of perceived proper diplomatic behavior dictated the nature of their reply.

There are no simple rules to prescribe for the U.S. in countering terrorism. The response to a fanatical terrorist group, a revolutionary movement using terrorist tactics, or international (i.e., governmental) terrorism may be very different. What is in vogue today for terrorists may be passé next year. The first hijacking, the first assassination, and the first kidnapping all garnered great attention. The wide scale coverage in the press tends to eventually make the events routine. Thus, new avenues of approach may be sought by terrorists to keep their group in the headlines. To date the U.S. government has responded by seeking to better its intelligence, harden its targets (better its security at embassies), develop contingency plans, develop effective methods of crisis management, and conclude various international agreements.

The fact that the U.S. has been spared significant terrorism on its soil makes the lobbying for funds difficult. The Department of the Treasury has had continuing difficulty in obtaining money for its Uniform Division. With the dearth of attacks against diplomatic missions in the Washington area, the need for a larger force has not been sufficiently demonstrated to OMB. In a time of budget cutting the combined efforts of State and Treasury brought forth the reply from OMB that the matter needed further study. However, should one or more embassies be successfully targeted by terrorists, it could be expected that monies would quickly become available.

One response to the problem of terrorism has been the call for a "counterterrorist czar" to be located in the White House. The thrust of the Omnibus Bill before the Ribicoff Committee on Governmental Affairs was in this direction. The term "czar" implies a strong element of control that would be, in fact, nonexistent. As was shown in this study, numerous federal agencies have statutory powers which dictate what their particular agency can and cannot do. Any czar would be constantly bound by these legalized institutionalized barriers and could only coordinate, never dictate.

The Interdepartmental Group on Terrorism, considering all that has been said so far, may be the only option available. However, it must be able to function in a cooperative fashion despite bureaucratic tendencies. To facilitate this there must be a clear and continuous mandate from the White House. The problem of terrorism must be viewed as ongoing and inimicable. The Interdepartmental Group must endeavor to study issues, domestically as well as internationally, prepare studies, and propose options for decision. Without the added weight from the White House, the group will fall short of effectively developing policy. Coordination alone is not enough. The direction and authority to implement must go hand in glove with any response.

This does not call for a very different structure than exists today. The organizational arrangement should encompass the present two track (law enforcement and diplomatic) framework. However, the group, whatever it be termed, must have the confidence of the president. Coupled with this would be the needed authority to direct the government response to any attack. Such a setup would facilitate presidential participation in an informed way, managing the action in lieu of only reacting to the threat.

A study of the Reagan administration through October 1981 sheds some light on this very aspect. In a review of the decision making process by correspondent Leslie H. Gelb (himself a former State department official), certain practices were made manifest.[1] The National Security Advisor and his assistants were seen as playing a secondary role and not the traditional role of coordinator of the various departmental views on an issue. A new National Security Planning Group, similar to the NSC without the presence of the chairman of the Joint Chiefs of Staff or any staff aides, was formed. The only members are the Vice President, the Secretary of State, Secretary of Defense, the director of the CIA, the chief counsellor to the president, the chief of the White House staff and his deputy, the National Security Advisor "as note-taker and participant." There is no memorandum that formally established the group. The purpose of the gathering is to create a collegial atmosphere as well as a balance of power among the principal advisors. The president and his top advisors and not the bureaucracy, would shape the issues and the timing in dealing with them. The much touted crisis management committee headed by the vice president was not convened until the end of the first year of the Reagan administration.

The article further indicated that the administration had not yet formally reviewed presidential decisions on almost every national security subject made by previous administrations. This leaves the bureaucracy lacking authoritative policy statements on a host of significant issues.

Preparations needed for the meetings at the White House are described as erratic. Apparently some papers are not prepared by the experts in the area of concern and at times they are prepared no more than twelve hours in advance of the meetings. One example cited noted that the National Security Planning Group "met in July (1981) to discuss terrorism and was given a paper that had not even been approved by the relevant assistant secretaries." This leads to the conclusion that White House meetings can occur without agreed papers by the experts in the particular fields. One of the great hazards of such a system as this, where subordinates rarely see minutes of what has been discussed or a memorandum on decisions, is that participants often are left with a number of conflicting interpretations of what happened and what has been decided. The article also indicated that officials opined that due to the lack of consistent guidance from the top, there had been endless wrangling on issues within the bureaucracy. The appointment of William Clark, close associate of President Reagan, as the National Security Advisor may have an impact in this regard.

In any terrorist incident, the group initiating the attack has the element of surprise on its side. The choice of time, place and weapons are theirs for the choosing. Statistics have shown that terrorism is a continuing problem, increasing in size and scope. J. Bower Bell has vividly portrayed the dilemma of the 1970s and the potential theater of the 1980s when he wrote:

> After a decade of dismal terror, there can be few left who are still innocent of the new politics of atrocity and the war waged by tiny "armies" of fanatics bearing strange devices. All now know the long and grotesque litany of massacre: Lod-Munich-Khartoum-Rome-Athens-Vienna. Now millions are familiar with the luminous dreams of the obscure South Moluccans and the strange Japanese Red Army, with the fantasies of the Hanafis and the Symbionese Liberation Army, and with the alphabet of death -- PFLP, FLQ, IRA. Carlos-the-Jackal is a media antihero, and Croatia is now found in the headlines instead of in stamp albums. Anyone can be a victim, can ride the wrong airline, take the wrong commuter train or

accept the wrong executive position abroad.
While opening mail, passing a foreign embassy, standing in an airport boarding line
or next to a car, or attending a diplomatic
reception, any of us may draw a 'winning'
lottery ticket in the terrorist game.[2]

NOTES

1. New York Times, October 19, 1981, p. 1.
2. J. Bowyer Bell, A Time of Terror (New York:
Basic Books, Inc., 1978), p. 263.

Bibliography

Books

Alexander, Yonah et al., eds. Control of Terrorism: International Documents. New York: Crane, Russak, 1979.

Alexander, Yonah et al., eds. Terrorism: Theory and Practice. Boulder, CO: Westview Press, 1979.

Alexander, Yonah and Kilmarx, eds. Political Terrorism and Business. New York: Praeger Publishers, 1979.

Allison, Graham and Stanton, Peter. Remaking Foreign Policy: The Organizational Connection. New York: Basic Books, 1976.

Allison, Graham T. Essence of Decision. Boston: Little, Brown, 1971.

Anthony, Robert N. and Herzlinger, Regina. Management Control in Nonprofit Organizations. Homewood, IL: Richard D. Irwin, Inc., 1975.

Bell, J. Bowyer. A Time of Terror. New York: Basic Books, 1978.

Blau, Peter and Scott, W. Richard. Formal Organizations: A Comparative Approach. San Francisco: Chandler Publishing Co., 1962.

Carlton, David and Schaerf, Carlo, eds. International Terrorism and World Security. New York: Wiley, 1978.

Cummings, L. L. and Scott, W. E., Jr., eds. Readings in Organizational Behavior and Human Performance. Homewood, IL: Richard D. Irwin, Inc., 1969.

Dobson, Christopher and Payne, Ronald. The Terrorists. New York: Facts on File, 1979.

Easton, David. Framework of Political Analysis. Englewood Cliffs, NJ: Prentice-Hall, 1965.

Endicott, John E. and Stafford, Roy W., eds. International Terrorism: A Balance Sheet. 4th ed. Baltimore: Johns Hopkins University Press, 1977.

Evans, Ernest. Calling a Truce to Terrorism. Westport, CT: Greenwood Press, 1979.

Gerth, H. H. and Mills, C. Wright, trans. and eds. From Max Weber: Essays in Sociology. New York: Oxford University Press, 1946.

Graham, Hugh Davis and Gurr, Ted Robert, eds. Violence in America. Beverly Hills, CA: Sage, 1979.

Hampton, David R., et al. Organizational Behavior and the Practice of Management. ILL: Scott, Foresman & Co., 1968.

Head, Richard G., et al. Crisis Resolution: Presidential Decision Making in the Mayaguez and Korean Confrontations. Boulder, CO: Westview Press, 1978.

130

Head, Richard G. and Rokke, Ervin J., eds. American Defense Policy. Baltimore: Johns Hopkins University Press, 1973.

Janis, Irving. Victims of Groupthink. Boston: Houghton Mifflin, 1972.

Laqueur, Walter, ed. The Terrorism Reader. New York: A Meridian Book, New American Library, 1978.

Lawless, David J. Organizational Behavior. Englewood Cliffs, NJ: Prentice-Hall, 1979.

Litterer, Joseph A. Analysis of Organizations. 2nd ed. New York: Wiley, 1973.

March, James G., ed. Handbook of Organizations. Chicago: Rand McNally, 1965.

March, James G. and Simon, Herbert A. Organizations. New York: Wiley, 1958.

Merton, Robert K. Social Theory and Social Structure. New York: Free Press, 1957.

Parry, Albert. Terrorism from Robespierre to Arafat. New York: Vanguard Press, 1976.

Parsons, Talcott. Structure and Process in Modern Societies. Glencoe, IL: Free Press, 1960.

Parsons, Talcott. Structure of Social Action. New York: Free Press, 1968.

Schreiber, Jan. The Ultimate Weapon: Terrorists and World Order. New York: Morrow, 1978.

Schultz, Richard H. and Sloan, Stephen, eds. Responding to the Terrorist Threat. New York: Pergamon Press, 1980.

Selznick, Philip. Leadership in Administration. New York: Harper & Row, 1957.

Simon, Herbert A. Administrative Behavior. New York: Free Press, 1976.

Taylor, Fredrick W. The Principles of Scientific Management. New York: Harper Bros., 1911.

Thompson, James C. Rolling Thunder. Chapel Hill: University of North Carolina Press, 1980.

Weber, Max. The Theory of Social and Economic Organizations. A. M. Henderson and Talcott Parsons, trans. T. Parsons, ed. Glencoe, IL: Free Press and Falcon's Wing Press, 1947.

Wilensky, Harold L. Organizational Intelligence. New York: Basic Books, 1967.

Articles, Journals, and Newspapers

Blau, Peter. "Organizations." International Encyclopedia of Social Sciences. v. 11. New York: Macmillan and Free Press, 1968.

Blumenthal, W. Michael. "Candid Reflections of a Businessman in Washington." Fortune, January 29, 1979.

Del Grosso, C. S. and Short, John C. "A Concept for Anti-
    terrorist Operations." Marine Corps Gazette, June,
    1979.
Dugard, John. "International Terrorism: Problems of
    Definition." International Affairs (London). v. 50,
    no. 1, January 1974.
Fromkin, David. "The Strategy of Terrorism." Foreign
    Affairs, v. 53, July, 1975.
Hardman, J. B. S. "Terrorism." The Encyclopedia of the
    Social Sciences. v. XIV. New York: Macmillan, 1964.
Hoffacher, Louis. "The U. S. Government Response to Ter-
    rorism." Vital Speeches of the Day, February 15,
    1975.
Korb, Lawrence J. "An Analysis of the Congressional
    Budget Act of 1974." Naval War College Review,
    Spring, 1977.
Leacocos, John. "Kissinger's Apparat." Foreign Policy,
    no. 5, 1971.
Meeks, Clarence I. "Illegal Law Enforcement: Aiding
    Civil Authorities in Violation of the Posse Com-
    itatus Act." Military Law Review, v. 70, Fall, 1975.
Newsweek, October 31, 1977.
Paust, Jordan J. "A Survey of Possible Legal Responses
    to International Terrorism: Prevention, Punishment,
    and Cooperative Action." Georgia Journal of Inter-
    national and Comparative Law, 1975.
Sloan, Stephen and Learney, Richard. "Non-Territorial
    Terrorism: An Empirical Approach to Policy Formula-
    tion.: Conflict, 1978.
U.S. News and World Report, September 1970.

                        Newspapers

"Desert One Revisited." The Washington Post, August 31,
    1980, p. D 6.
New York Times, March 10, 1977; July 15, 22, 1977; April
    23, 1978; November 4, 1979; December 9, 1979; May
    11, 1980; June 10, 1980; January 28, 1981; February
    3, 1981.
Washington Post, January 29, 1981.

                  U.S. Government Documents

Public Law 93-366, Antihijacking Act and Air Transporta-
    tion Security Act, 93rd Congress, S. 39, August 5,
    1974.
U.S. Central Intelligence Agency. Central Intelligence
    Agency Fact Book. Washington: n.d.
        . International and Transnational Terrorism:
    Diagnosis and Prognosis, by David L. Milbank. Re-
    search Study PR 76 10030. Washington: April 1976.

U.S. Congress. House. Committee on International Rela-
tions. Subcommittee on International Security and
Scientific Affairs. International Terrorism: Leg-
islative Initiatives. Hearing on H. R. 13387.
September 12, 1978.
_____. _____. Committee on the Judiciary.
Federal Capabilities in Crises Management and Ter-
rorism. Staff Report. Subcommittee on Civil and
Constitutional Rights. 95th Congress, 2nd session,
December 1978.
_____. _____. _____. _____. Hear-
ings before a subcommittee of the Committee on the
Judiciary. House of Representatives. 95th Congress,
2nd session, 1978.
_____. Senate. Committee on Governmental Affairs.
An Act to Combat International Terrorism. Hearings
before the main committee. S2236. 95th Congress,
2nd session, 1978.
_____. _____. _____. _____. Staff
Report S2236, 95th Congress, 2nd session, 1978.
_____. _____. Committee on the Judiciary. Sub-
committee of the Committee of the Judiciary. Terror-
istic Activity, International Terrorism. 94th Con-
gress, 1st session, May 14, 1975.
U.S. Constitution, Article 2, Section 3; Article 4,
Section 4; and Article 14, Section 1.
U.S Department of the Army. DA Civil Disturbance Plan
(Garden Plot). Headquarters. Washington: August 3,
1978.
United States Code. Congressional and Administrative News.
94th Congress, vols. 2-4, 1976.
U.S. Department of Energy. "DOE Safeguards on Nuclear
Materials Facilities." Fact Sheet. Washington:
Office of Public Affairs, July 1978.
_____. Order 5632.2, February 16, 1979.
U.S. Department of State. Bulletin. Washington: October
23, 1972; March 26, 1973; September 15, 1975;
October 6, 1975; October 11, 1976; March 1978;
September 1979.
_____. Newsletter. Washington: April 1973, Aug-
ust-September 1976.
U.S. Energy Research and Development Administration
(now part of DOE). "Safeguards." Fact Sheet.
Washington: ERDA, October 1978.
U.S. Laws, Statutes, etc. U.S. Code, Title 10, Sections
331, 332, 333. Washington: U.S. Govt. Print. Off.,
1973.
United States Government Manual 1979-1980. Washington:
U.S. Govt. Print. Off., May 1979.

International Government Organizations

United Nations. Yearbook of the United Nations: 1970.
New York: U.N. Office of Public Information, 1971.

Published Reports

Center for Policy Research. National Governors' Assoc-
iation. Domestic Terrorism. Washington: U.S. Govt.
Print. Off., May 1979.
deLeon, Peter, et al. Attributes of Potential Criminal
Adversaries of U.S. Nuclear Programs. R-2225-SL.
Santa Monica, CA: The Rand Corporation, February
1978.
Executive Committee on Terrorism. The United States
Government Antiterrorist Program. Washington:
National Security Council, June 1979.
International Association of Chiefs of Police, Inc.
Final Report. Needs Assessment Study: Terrorism
in Dade County, Florida. Miami, FL: Dade-Miami
Criminal Justice Council, July 1979.
Jenkins, Brian M. and Johnson, Janera. International
Terrorism: A Chronology, 1968-1974. R-1597-
DOS/ARPA. Santa Monica, CA: The Rand Corporation,
1975.
Jenkins, Brian M. International Terrorism: A New Kind
of Warfare. Report P-5216. Santa Monica, CA: The
Rand Corporation, June 1974.
Kupperman, Robert H. Facing Tomorrow's Terrorist Inci-
dent Today. Law Enforcement Assistance Administra-
tion. U.S. Department of Justice. Washington:
October 1977.
Risks International. Executive Risk Assessment. v. I,
no. 8, Alexandria, VA: June 1979.
_____. Executive Risk Assessment. v. I, no. 12,
Alexandria, VA: 1979.
_____. North America. Alexandria, VA: August 1979.

Unpublished Reports/Letters/Interviews/Memos

Bunce, Joseph. "Crime in the Streets: A National Policy
Issue." Unpublished Paper, undated.
Holloway, James L., III. "Rescue Mission Report."
Report prepared for the Joint Chiefs of Staff, Aug-
ust 1980.
Interview with John N. Gatch, former Deputy Special Assis-
tant to Combat Terrorism, Department of State: Jan-
uary 24, 1980, December 9, 1980.
Interview with Franklin D. Kramer, Assistant Secretary
for International Security Affairs, Department of
Defense, December 2, 1980.

134

Interview with Robert H. Kupperman, Georgetown Center for
    International Studies: January 22, 1980.
Interview with Thomas Love, Special Agent, FBI, Ann Arbor,
    MI: July 1979.
Interview with Commander A. Robert Matt, Intelligence and
    Security Division, U.S. Coast Guard: June 11, 1980.
Interview with Robert McBrien, Office of the Assistant
    Secretary for Enforcement and Operations, U.S.
    Department of the Treasury, Washington: February
    13, 1980, November 17, 1980.
Interviews -- Several interviews were conducted with per-
    sonnel currently or formerly affiliated with the Cab-
    inet Committee to Combat Terrorism and its Working
    Group, and the Executive Committee and its Working
    Group. Additionally, House and Senate staff members
    who participated in various hearings were interviewed.
    Their comments were provided on a non-attribution
    basis. The interviews were conducted on the following
    dates: January 17, 12, 26, 1980; January 28, 1980;
    February 22, 1980; February 24-29, 1980; June 6,
    9, 1980; November 14, 1980; December 4, 5, 16, 1980;
    December 16, 1980; December 19, 1980; January 13,
    1981.
Letter from Douglas J. Bennet, Jr., Assistant Secretary
    for Congressional Relations, to Don Edwards, House
    of Representatives, December 14, 1978.
Letter from John L. Naler to Senator Abe Ribicoff to
    Harold Brown, May 7, 1979.
Memo from Zbigniew Brzezinski supplementing his September
    16, 1977 memo establishing the NSC/SCC Working Group
    on Terrorism, October 20, 1977.
Memorandum, Harold Brown, Secretary of Defense. "Estab-
    lishment of a DOD Counter-Terrorism Steering Commit-
    tee," January 9, 1978.
Memorandum of Understanding between the Department of
    Transportation and Department of Defense, signed
    August 7, 1978, and September 7, 1978.
Memorandum of Understanding between the Director, FBI,
    and the Commandant, USCG, signed March 23, 1979,
    and April 17, 1979.
Rabe, Robert L. "Crisis Management of Terrorist Inci-
    dents: Legal Aspects and Issues." Unpublished
    paper, copyright 1979 by author.

Index

Abductions. See Hijackings;
    Hostages; Kidnappings
"Act for the Prevention and
    Punishment of Crimes Against
    Internationally Protected
    Persons" (P.L. 94-467), 87
Africa, 77, 81, 82
Agencies. See Government
    Organizations
AIM. See American Indian
    Movement
Air Force, 61. See also Armed
    forces
Air Line Pilots Association, 109
Air Transportation Security Act.
    See Antihijacking Act
Alexander I (king of
    Yugoslavia), 7
Allison, Graham T., 25
Alon, Yosef, 77
American Indian Movement (AIM),
    66(n18)
Antihijacking Act (P.L. 93-366),
    87, 101, 108
Armed forces
  capabilities, 59-65, 122
  civilian control of, 50-51,
    53-54
  demographics of, 49-50
  domestic terrorism and, 49-68
  equipment loans, 54-55, 57,
    67(n21)
  legal restraints upon, 52-59
  order of deployment, 57
  politics and, 51-52
  presidential control over,
    53-54
  public perception of, 49-50

  as target, 79, 81
  See also Department of Defense;
    names of particular branches
Armed Forces of National Libera-
    tion, 70
Armenians, 70
Arms Control and Disarmament
    Agency, 31(n29), 37
Army
  Delta Team, 65
  Ranger Batallions, 60, 63
  Special Forces, 61
  See also Armed forces; Department
    of the Army
Aron, David, 113
Asia, 77, 81
Assassinations, 72(Table 6.2),
    92(n2)
Atomic Energy Act, 46
Attorney General, 58, 104
Austria, 9
Authority structures, 1, 5(n3)
Automatic weapons, 83

Baader-Meinof Gang, 89
BATF. See Bureau of Alcohol,
    Tobacco, and Firearms
Beckwith, Charles, 62
Bell, Griffin, 91, 94(n39)
Bell, J. Bower, 127
Biological weapons, 83
Black Guerilla Family, 70
Black Panther Party, 70
Black September Organization (BSO),
    70, 77, 88-90
"Blue Light," 62
Bombings, 70, 74(Table 6.4), 81
Bombs, 82

Border Protection Group Nine.
See Grenzschutzgruppe-9
Brazil, 16(n18)
Brown, Harold, 108, 109
Brzezinski, Zbigniew, 36, 112,
113
BSO. See Black September
Organization
Bureau of Alcohol, Tobacco, and
Firearms (BATF), 45, 46, 102
Bureau of Intelligence and
Research, 44
Business
as target, 70, 79, 81, 82,
92(n2), 94(n35)

Cabinet Committee to Combat
Terrorism, 20, 41, 88, 96
mandate of, 32-33
policy guidelines, 33-34
Carter, Jimmy, 88, 106
antiterrorist program, 34-35,
38(Fig. 4.1), 39(Fig. 4.2),
62, 90
CIA and, 44
domestic crime and, 107
ECT and, 114
Warrensville Heights incident
and, 90
Washington incident and, 91
Castro, Fidel, 100
Central America. See Latin America
Central Intelligence Agency (CIA),
44, 110
Chemical weapons, 83
China. See People's Republic of
China
CIA. See Central Intelligence
Agency
Civiletti, Benjamin R., 26,
47(n10)
"Civil Violence and the Process
of Development," 5(n4)
Clark, William, 127
Classical administrative
theory, 22
Coast Guard (USCG), 45, 99, 101-
102
Posse Comitatus Act and, 52-53
Colombia, 79
Committee on Governmental
Affairs, 59, 125
Communications Operations

Center, 43
Congress
president and, 51, 85-87
role of, 85-88, 92(n13)
Constitution
armed forces and, 53-54
Contingency Planning and Crisis
Management Committee
(Foreign and Domestic), 42,
98, 105
Convention Against Taking Hostages,
9-10
Convention for the Prevention and
Punishment of Terrorism, 7
Convention for the Suppression of
Unlawful Acts Against the
Safety of Civil Aviation, 8
Convention on Offenses and Certain
Other Acts Committed on Board
Aircraft, 8
Convention on the Prevention and
Punishment of Crimes Against
Internationally Protected
Persons Including Diplomatic
Agents, 9, 58
Conventions, 8-10
Convention to Prevent and Punish
Acts of Terrorism Taking the
Form of Crimes Against Persons
and Related Extortion that are
of International Significance,
9, 58
Council for Combating Terrorism, 86
Counter-Terrorism Steering
Committee, 108-109
Croatians, 70
hijackings by (1976, 1978), 90,
94(n36)
Crozier, Brian, 15(n15), 16(n27)
Cuban National Liberation Front,
70
Cuban refugees
hijackings by, 100
Cubans, 70, 100
Customs Service, 45, 100, 102,
103-104
Cyprus incident (1978), 59

Davis, Benjamin O., 100
Decentralization, 3-4
Declaration of Principles of Inter-
national Law Concerning
Friendly Relations and

Cooperation Among States
(U.N.), 7-8
DeCourcy, William P., 115(n22)
Defense Intelligence Agency, 44
Department of Commerce, 110
Department of Defense (DOD), 44,
55, 59, 65, 100, 122
FBI and, 57
jurisdiction of, 107-110
See also Armed forces,
Posse Comitatus Act
Department of Energy (DOE), 44,
46
jurisdiction of, 110-111
Department of Energy Organization
Act, 110
Department of Housing and Urban
Development, 110
Department of Justice (DOJ), 26,
43-44, 55, 57, 86
Department of State and, 105,
123
jurisdiction of, 35-36,
104-107, 114
See also Attorney General;
Contingency Planning and
Crisis Management Committee;
Federal Bureau of Investi-
gation; Law Enforcement
Assistance Administration;
Security Policy Committee
Department of State, 43, 58, 86,
121
Department of Justice and,
105, 123
ECT Working Group and, 113
Iran mission and, 124
jurisdiction of, 35, 96-99,
114
Secret Service and, 102
See also Interdepartmental
Group on Terrorism; Office
for Combatting Terrorism
Department of the Army
Civil Disturbance Plan, 56-57,
59
See also Army
Department of the Interior, 110
Department of the Navy, 110.
See also Navy
Department of the Treasury,
44, 45-46, 122, 125
Assistant Secretary for

Enforcement and Operations, 102
jurisdiction of, 102-104
See also Customs Service; Secret
Service
Department of Transportation, 45,
122
jurisdiction of, 99-102
See also Antihijacking Act;
Federal Aviation Administration;
International Civil Aviation
Organization
Deterrence, 33, 35, 65, 90
Diplomats. See Protected persons
DOD. See Department of Defense
DOE. See Department of Energy
DOJ. See Department of Justice
Drug Enforcement Administration, 44

ECT. See Executive Committee on
Terrorism
Edwards, Don, 37, 40
Egypt, 59
Eid, Guy, 89
El Salvador, 79
Emergency Program Center, 104-105
Energy Reorganization Act, 46
Energy Research and Development
Administration (ERDA), 37, 110
Entebbe incident (1976), 59
Environmental Protection Agency, 26
ERDA. See Energy Research and
Development Administration
Europe, 69, 70, 77, 81, 82, 92(n2)
European Convention on the
Suppression of Terrorism, 9,
16(n22)
Executive Committee on Terrorism
(ECT), 36, 47(n5), 59, 96, 114,
123-124
Working Group, 36-37, 39(Fig. 4.2),
40-46, 96-98, 103, 105, 106,
112-113, 122-123
Working Group committees, 42-43
Executive Protection Service. See
Secret Service, Uniform
Division
Extortion, 83-84

Facility attacks, 76(Table 6.6),
81-82, 84, 92(n2)
DOE and, 110-111
FBI. See Federal Bureau of
Investigation

Fearey, Robert A., 40-41, 97, 113
Federal Aviation Administration,
    45, 87, 94(n36), 99-101, 103,
    108, 109
  jurisdiction of, 36, 44
Federal Bureau of Investigation
    (FBI), 23-24, 43-44, 58,
    94(n36), 101-102, 104, 108,
    109
  armed forces and, 56-57
  jurisdiction of, 36
Federal Energy Administration,
    110
Federal Law Enforcement Training
    Center, 102
Federal Power Commission, 110
Federal Republic of Germany.
    See German Federal Republic
Ford, Gerald R., 90, 115(n22)
Foreign Relations Committee, 87
France, 9, 60

"Garbage can theory," 31(n41)
Garden Plot. See Department of
    the Army, Civil Disturbance
    Plan
Gatch, John A., 97
Gelb, Leslie H., 126
George Jackson Brigade, 70
German Federal Republic, 9,
    17(n28), 31(n27), 59, 60, 89,
    94(n35)
Gigene (France), 60
Glenn, John, 59
Government
  as target, 79, 81
Governmental Affairs Committee,
    85. See also Committee on
    Governmental Affairs
Government organizations, 1, 3-4,
    21, 38-39(Fig. 4.1, 4.2),
    42-46, 121-122, 122-123
  changes in, 23-24, 27-28
  inaction of, 4, 5(n4)
  jurisdictions of, 96-118
  nature of, 28-29
  rivalry among, 28
  See also Cabinet Committee to
    Combat Terrorism; Department
    of Defense; Department of
    State; Executive Committee
    on Terrorism; National
    Security Council; Office for

Combatting Terrorism
Grant, Ulysses S., 52
Grenzschutzgruppe-9 (G.S.G.-9)
    (W. Germany), 59, 62, 65
G.S.G.-9. See Grenzschutzgruppe-9
Guatemala, 79

Hague Convention, 8
Haig, Alexander M., Jr., 46, 99
Hanafi Moslems, 91
Hayden, Tom, 2
Hearst, Patty, 14(n2), 120
Heck, L. Douglas, 97
Hijackings, 8, 45, 75(Table 6.5),
    87, 99-101
  DOD and, 109
  See also Hostages; Kidnappings
Hoffacker, Lewis, 37, 97, 113
Holloway, James L., III, 24, 63
Holloway Report, 24, 26-27
Hostages, 9-10
  negotiating for, 31(n36)
  See also Hijackings; Kidnappings
Human rights, 2, 4(n2), 8, 119
Huntington, Samuel, 5(n4), 51
Hurwitz, Edward, 97

Immigration and Nationality Act,
    107
Immigration and Naturalization
    Service, 43, 107
Independent Armed Revolutionary
    Commandos, 70
Intelligence gathering, 47(n10)
Interdepartmental Group on
    Terrorism, 46, 123, 124, 126
International Association of Chiefs
    of Police, Inc., 16(n25)
International Civil Aviation
    Organization, 33, 45
International Initiatives
    Committee, 42-43
Interstate Commerce Commission, 110
IRA. See Irish Republican Army
Iran, 18(n33)
  hostage rescue attempt, 24, 26-27,
    63-64, 124
Irish Republican Army (IRA), 70, 77
Isham, Heyward, 97
Israel, 15(n16), 59, 89, 99
Italy, 9, 17(n28), 83, 92(n2)

Japan, 5(n3), 17(n28), 94(n35), 125

Japanese Red Army, 5(n3), 77, 125

Javits, Jacob, 87

Jenkins, Brian M., 15(n16), 17(n32)

Jewish Defense League, 70

Jordan, 89

Karkashian, John E., 97

Kelley, Clarence, 91

Kennedy, Richard T., 99

Khartoum incident (1973), 88-90

Kidnappings, 73(Table 6.3), 81, 92(n2), 94(n35). See also Hijackings; Hostages

Kissinger, Henry, 90, 112

Kupperman, Robert H., 106

Lally, Richard, 100

Latin America, 69, 70, 77, 79, 81

Law Enforcement Assistance Administration (LEAA), 43, 102, 105-107

LEAA. See Law Enforcement Assistance Administration

League of Nations, 7

Lebanon, 17(n28)

Libya, 83

Lod Airport incident (1972), 15(n16), 17(n28), 32

Lombroso, Cesare, 7

Macomer, William B., Jr., 89

Mao Tse-tung, 90

Marine Corps

Battalion Landing Team, 60

Force Reconnaissance Company, 61

Marine Amphibious Unit, 60

See also Armed forces

McGiffert, David E., 59, 61, 63

Media, 2, 13(n2), 119-120, 124

Memorandum of Understanding between the Director, Federal Bureau of Investigation, and the Commandant, United States Coast Guard, 101-102

Mexico, 16(n18)

Meyer, Armin H., 33, 96-97, 112, 113

Middle East, 81

Military capabilities. See Armed forces, capabilities

Miller, G. William, 103

Missiles. See Precision-Guided Munitions

Modernization, 5(n4)

Mogadishu incident (1976), 59, 60

Montreal Convention, 8

Moore, George, 89

Munich Olympics incident (1972), 32, 88

Muskie, Edmund, 103

National Foreign Intelligence Program, 44

National Security Advisor, 126

National Security Agency, 44

National Security Council (NSC), 4, 35-36, 88, 124

jurisdiction of, 111-114

See also Executive Committee on Terrorism; Presidential Review Memorandum No. 30; Special Coordination Committee

National Security Planning Group, 126, 127

Navy

Posse Comitatus Act and, 52-53

Sea, Air, Land Platoons (SEAL), 61

See also Armed forces; Department of the Navy

NEST. See Nuclear Emergency Search Team

New World Liberation Front, 70

New York City blackout, 3, 119

Nixon, Richard M., 20

Cabinet Committee to Combat Terrorism memorandum, 32, 41, 88, 96, 98

ECT Working Group and, 112, 113

hijackings and, 99

Khartoum incident and, 89

Noel, Cleo A., 89

Norway, 9

NRC. See Nuclear Regulatory Commission

NSC. See National Security Council

Nuclear devices, 82-83, 83-85, 110

fuel cycle process and, 84

Nuclear Emergency Search Team (NEST), 46

Nuclear facilities

Nuclear facilities (cont)
  materials loss, 84
Nuclear Regulatory Commission
    (NRC), 46, 111

Office for Combatting Terrorism,
    43, 86, 97, 98, 99, 121-122,
    123, 124
Office of Civil Aviation Security,
    100
Office of Justice Assistance,
    Research and Statistics
    (OJARS), 107
Office of Law Enforcement
    Assistance, 106. See also
    Law Enforcement Assistance
    Administration
Office of Management and Budget
    (OMB)
  Secret Service and, 103, 125
Office of Safeguards and
    Security, 46
Office of Transportation
    Security, 100
Oil platforms
  as target, 101
OJARS. See Office of Justice
    Assistance, Research and
    Statistics
OMB. See Office of Management
    and Budget
Omega 7, 70
Omnibus Antiterrorism Act, 59,
    104
Omnibus Crime Control and Safe
    Streets Act, 105
Organizational structure, 25
Organization for Antiterrorism
    Planning, Coordination,
    and Policy Formulation,
    39(Fig. 4.2)
Organization for Response to
    Terrorist Incidents, 38
    (Fig. 4.1)
Organization of American
    States
  Convention, 9, 58
Organizations, 19-31
  contingency plans in, 27
  decision making in, 24-25
  goals in, 22-24, 30(n19)
  government. See Government
    organizations

literature of, 19
  multiple perspectives in, 25-26
  nature of, 20-22
  problem factoring in, 25, 31(n27)
  public. See Government organi-
    zations
  standard operating procedures, 26
  terrorist. See Terrorist
    organizations
  theory of, 21-22
  vesting interests in, 26
Organized anarchy theory. See
    "Garbage can theory"

Palestinians, 15(n16), 17(n28),
    70, 88-90, 99
Parsons, Talcott, 19
People's Republic of China, 5(n4)
PFLP. See Popular Front for the
    Liberation of Palestine
PGMs. See Precision-Guided
    Munitions
Police
  as target, 79, 81
Policy Review Committee (PRC), 35
Political systems, 4(n2)
Popular Front for the Liberation
    of Palestine (PFLP), 17(n28),
    99
Portugal, 9
Posse Comitatus Act, 44, 52-53,
    54, 55-56, 57, 60, 66-67(n21)
  exceptions to, 57-59
PRC. See Policy Review Committee
Precision-Guided Munitions (PGMs),
    82
Prediction, 35
President
  as commander in chief, 52-53
  congress and, 51, 85-87
  role of, 88-91, 104, 124
Presidential Review Memorandum
    No. 30, 35, 86, 87, 88, 98,
    105, 106, 108, 111, 113-114
Press. See Media
Prevention, 34
PRM 30. See Presidential Review
    Memorandum No. 30
Protected persons, 9, 58-59, 87,
    102-103, 115(n22)
Public Information Committee, 42
Public Law 91-644, 58-59
Public Law 93-366, 87

Public Law 94-467, 87
Puerto Ricans, 2, 70

Quainton, Anthony C. E., 35,
    40, 97-98
Quebec Liberation Front, 69

Radio. See Media
Ransoms, 73(Table 6.3), 81,
    94(n35)
Reaction, 35
Reagan, Ronald, 20, 96, 99
    antiterrorism program, 46, 65,
        88, 91, 126-127
    Department of Justice under,
        43, 104
Red Brigade, 83
Red Feather. See United States
    vs. Red Feather
Red Guerrilla Family, 70
Research and Development
    Committee, 42
Research and Special Programs
    Directorate, 100
Resource Conservation and
    Recovery Act, 26
Revolutionary Communist Party, 70
Ribicoff, Abraham, 86-87, 109,
    111, 125
Risks International, Inc.,
    91-92(n1)
Rivkind, Perry, 37, 40
Rogers, William, 32, 96, 112,
    113

Sabotage, 8
Saiyeret (Israel), 59
Sam Melville-Jonathan Jackson
    Unit, 70
SAS. See Special Air Service
SA-7 (Soviet missile), 82
SCC. See Special Coordination
    Committee
Schaefer, Edward, 97
Scientific management movement,
    22
SDS. See Students for a
    Democratic Society
SEAL. See Navy, Sea, Air, Land
    Platoons
Secret Service, 41, 45
    Uniform Division, 41, 102-103,
        115(n22), 125

Security maintenance, 1
Security Policy Committee
    (Domestic), 42, 98, 105
Security Policy Committee
    (Foreign), 42
Self-determination, 8
Senate, 59. See also Governmental
    Affairs Committee; Committee
    on Governmental Affairs
Senate Bill 2236, 85, 86-87
Serbians, 70
Simon, Herbert A., 23
Sirhan, Sirhan, 89
Sky marshal program, 99-100
SOPs. See Organizations, standard
    operating procedures
Sourwine, J. G., 40-41
South America, 81
Soviet Union, 9
Spain, 79, 92(n2)
Special Air Service (SAS)
    (Britain), 60, 65
Special Coordination Committee
    (SCC), 35-36, 39(Fig. 4.2),
    88, 111
Squadra Anti-Commando (Italy), 60
Statistics, 69-82
Students for a Democratic Society
    (SDS), 2
Sudan, 88-90
Sweden, 9
Symbionese Liberation Army, 2,
    13-14(n2), 70
Syria, 17(n28)

Technology
    terrorist targets and, 3
Television. See Media
Terror, 10-11
Terrorism
    activity rates, 4(n1), 69-70,
        71(Table 6.1), 77, 78(Table 6.7),
        79, 80(Table 6.8)
    coercive, 15(n15)
    definition of, 6-7, 10-12, 16(n25),
        17-18(n32), 67(n24), 121
    disruptive, 15(n15)
    domestic, 13
    international, 12, 17(n29), 77
    motives for, 10, 121
    nature of, 120-121, 125
    nonterritorial, 13
    transnational, 12-13, 17(n29)

Terrorism (cont)
  typology, 70, 72-76(Tables 6.2-
    6.6)
"Terrorist international," 12,
  17(n28)
Terrorist organizations
  foreign-based, 70, 77
  See also names of particular
  organizations
Third World, 82
Tokyo Convention, 8
Tucker, Roy, 91(n1)

United Nations, 7-8
  Convention, 9, 58
United States vs. Red Feather,
  54-55, 56, 67(n21)
USGC. See Coast Guard
Utilities. See Facility attacks

Values, 2, 4(n2), 119
  instrumental vs. terminal, 24
Vance, Cyrus, 86

Vulnerability, 119
  urban, 3

War Powers Resolution, 51
Warrensville Heights incident
  (1977), 90
Washington incident (1978), 91,
  94-95(n39)
Weapons, 82-83
Weathermen, 2. See also Weather
  Underground
Weather Underground, 70
Weber, Max, 19, 21-22
Wegener, Ulrich, 60
Weinberger, Caspar W., 65, 109
West Germany. See German Federal
  Republic
Working Group on Terrorism. See
  Executive Committee on
  Terrorism
Wounded Knee incident (1973),
  54-56, 66(n18), 66-67(n21)

Yugoslavia, 7